Dan Ch. Christensen

The Crash

Dan Ch. Christensen

THE CRASH

*The story of seven RAF-flyers' escape after
the shooting down of a Halifax aircraft in 1945
in Denmark told by five of them*

*In Denmark it paid to emphasize that
Denmark's struggle was a Danish show entirely, for which
SOE was providing the tools, liaison officers, communications,
and directives.
Even though this line was sometimes taken with 'the tongue in the cheek'
it paid never to hint that SOE was in control.*

Major Alistair Garrett in
Special Operations Executive's final report,
'History of the Danish Country Section', 1945.

The Crash
Published by Friends of the Danish Resistance Museum Publishing
Layout: Kjeld Thorsen and Narayana Press
Proofreading: Ole Rottbøll Westrup/Esben Kjeldbæk
Photos have kindly been made available by several sources
Illustration front-page: The Crew from the Halifax Aircraft, private archive

© 2000 Dan Charly Christensen
Friends of the Danish Resistance Museum Publishing

ISBN 87-88214-605
ISSN 87-0107-9298

Contents

Preface

Wednesday 14th February 1945 a RAF Halifax bomber took off from its base in Yorkshire, England, heading across the North Sea towards occupied Denmark.

The Halifax was loaded with mines to be dropped in the Bay of Stettin, Germany.

On board the Halifax were seven crew members: Johnny, the pilot, 'Red-Berry', the navigator, Andy, the wireless operator, Stan, the bomb aimer, Roy, the mechanic, and the two air gunners, Jimmy in the mid-upper turret, and Jim in the rear-turret.

Suddenly a German night-fighter appeared from behind firing at the Halifax.

This is the dramatic story of the shooting down of the Halifax and the destiny of the crew in German-occupied Denmark ....

THE CRASH

WEDNESDAY 14TH – DAY ONE

At 8.30 p.m. on Wednesday, the 14th February, 1945, Johannes Helms, a smallholder, was on his way home on his bicycle from Holbæk to Havremarken, when he observed a strange looking luminous tail of fire. It was traversing the sky from east to west, and approaching a position close to his home. It illuminated the landscape enabling him to see miles around, almost as if it were daylight. Only when the object was immediately above his head did he realise that it was an aircraft ablaze. A few minutes later, he also heard the air-raid warning hooting from Holbæk, the nearest town five or six miles away. Then suddenly the aircraft exploded in the air and fell out of the clouds trailing a plume of mourning black. Its parts were dispersed over a vast area. The fuselage of the aircraft crashed close to Søgaard, an old peoples' home, and an unexploded mine dropped from the aircraft and landed in the middle of the courtyard. The ground shuddered, and the old people panicked at what they believed to be an earthquake. Quite a few window panes and tiles were broken. Quickly, Helms biked to the site, but by now the flash had faded out and in the pitch-dark he found no surviving airmen.

Four-engine RAF-bomber shot down by the Luftwaffe.
Source: Luftwaffe's journal SIGNAL, 8,1944, p.7.

Other local people had been alerted by the flash, too, and walked out in the muddy fields carrying carbide lamps to see what had happened. Most farmhouses at that time had no electricity nor were batteries for torchlights available. Besides, the Germans had ordered a general blackout. Some families were too scared to break the curfew let alone open their door to somebody knocking. Others were unable to withstand the temptation of getting out there to look for something of value they could snatch away under the very noses of the Germans.

Rev. Paul With Johannesen, the local clergyman, had been listening to the news in Danish from the BBC when the white tower of Sønder Asmindrup church just outside his vicarage had reflected the bright flare of the explosion. Being a member of an illegal network whose task it was to assist allied airmen to escape, he jumped on his bike to look for survivors. Sadly, all he found was a dead body.

Soon after, however, a patrol of German *Feldwebel* (Military Police) arrived. They were probably the small group of observers from the German air defence warning service stationed at Mørkemosebjerg, about a mile away which, at the highest point in the neighbourhood, 106 metres, was suitable for an antenna mast. They had occupied an old farmhouse opposite their small bunker. The locals remember that these observers used to be well provided with Danish female company. Later, more German patrols arrived from Holbæk. The curious locals were pushed aside, and like Helms, Rev. Johannesen had to return home no wiser.

The aircraft, now irrefutably rendered harmless, had been a Halifax bomber – B.Mk.III MZ793 (ZA-X) – from RAF 10 squadron. Together with bombers from several other squadrons it had taken off from its home base at Melbourne, Yorkshire, and left the British coast at Flamborough Head on a filthy, miserable night. The usual spirited light banter was somehow missing that night and this was not helped by the bad weather. The stream of bombers had been flying low, at 500 feet, across the North Sea to avoid German radar, but when crossing the coastline of Jutland they had climbed to 10,000 feet and, soon after, further up to 16,000 feet to make themselves less vulnerable in case of flak.

At this point Andy, the wireless operator, noted flak on the starboard side of the aircraft. One of his duties was to observe the radar screen

Halifaxes of 10 Squadron on a sortie from Melbourne, Yorkshire. RAF 10 Sqn. was operational in Bomber Command throughout the war. By May '45 this squadron had received 9 Distinguished Service Orders, 333 Distinguished Flying Crosses, and 173 Distinguished Flying Medals.
Source: Yorkshire Air Museum, Elvington, York.

known as 'the fishpond' which was connected to the radar scanner (H2S). A *fishpond* was able to distinguish friend from foe. As opposed to the concentration of aircraft within the bomber stream moving at approximately the same speed, attacking fighters were readily discernible by their relatively rapid movement across the screen. Above Sjællands Odde Andy had observed two German night fighters on a parallel course and informed his pilot and two gunners accordingly. As the enemy was closing in fast the pilot was instructed to take evasive action and corkscrew to port which he did with quite a violent manoeuvre. At this stage the gunners believed they had shaken the enemy off.

However, this was not so. One of the Germans had pursued the Halifax after its evasive action and after about 25 miles he intercepted the

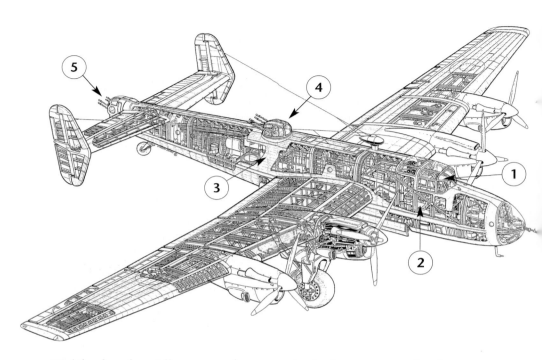

Halifax bomber. All crewmembers were in the front, except the air gunners, Jim, who was in the rear turret, and Jimmy, who was in the mid-upper turret.
Source: Victor F. Bingham, Halifax Second to None. The Handley Page Halifax, Airlife England, 1986.

Halifax for a second time. The ensuing air duel was observed from the ground by 17-year-old Herlev Hjortholm Nielsen, a farm boy at 'Hjortholmsgaarden'. He was alerted by the staggering noise of machine guns firing in space 16,000 feet almost exactly above his parents' farm. The night fighter had flown under the bomber into a position, which was most favourable for targeting the enemy and at the same time invulnerable to itself. Herlev now watched the mid-upper gunner and rear-gunner trying to engage the fighter in a counter attack. But the backfire

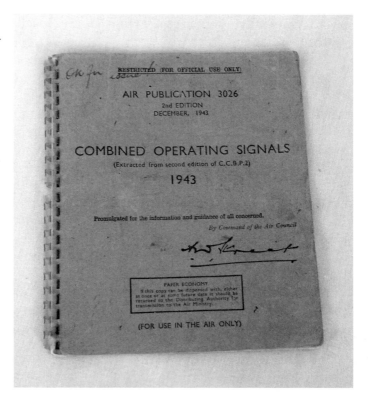

RAF Signal Book, Air Publication 3026, 2nd Edition, December, 1943, belonged to Andy, found at 'Hjortholmsgaarden', February, '45. Source: private archive

was of no avail. As Herlev heard the fighter leaving the air space towards southeast he could not help watching the tail of fire emanating from the left wing of the Halifax while a big sheet of metal landed right in front of him. The next morning he found Andy's signal book on his field.

When, for the second time, the pilot found evasive action the only way out he realized that his port engine was already hit. Indeed, the German volley had changed a magnificent means of airborne transport into a paralysed furnace bound to explode at any moment. Consequently, in order to lower the risk of the fire spreading, Johnny manoeuvred sharply to the starboard side while diving steeply. In fact he had turned his course by 180°. By this time Jim, the rear-gunner, had realized from his point of vantage that the game was up. Hence he baled out at about

10,000 feet at the moment the Halifax turned back into the direction from whence it had come.

From his position Andy, the wireless operator, heard the ear-splitting noise from the German machine gun. He could see that one wing was well alight. Flames shot way beyond the turret and it was quite obvious that the RAF bomber would explode at any second. So Andy took the precaution of clipping on his parachute pack. Roy, the flight engineer, was making his log out when suddenly he saw a blinding flash followed by a terrific bang. He looked through the astrodome to see what damage had been done and he, too, saw a fire begin on the port wing in the centre and rear behind the inboard engine. The engineer tried to feather the port engines to prevent the propellers from igniting the 'dead' engines thereby causing an explosion. He activated the engine fire extinguishers, but it was like putting out a burning house with a water pistol. The flames had enveloped the whole wing, so the pilot ordered his crew to prepare to bale out. An emergency landing was completely out of the question. Roy helped the pilot to put his parachute on and put on his own as well. Now the order 'Bale out!' was heard, and Roy went down to the front escape hatch, under the navigator's table, but found that the door was jammed or frozen.

During the almost vertical spiral dive moving inside the aircraft was extremely difficult. Stan, the bomb aimer, was thrown over the bomb sight into the nose of the aircraft, and Andy was thrown to the floor. Jimmy, the mid-upper gunner, having left his turret was pushed back to the rear of the aircraft. Then an almighty noise was heard and there was a tearing of metal. The bomber was blown to pieces at the height of only a few thousand feet and scraps of metal were being dispersed over a vast area. Stan and Andy were flung out of the shattered fuselage instantly. Roy, too, was yanked out in a state of unconsciousness and only came to his senses while floating down to earth with an open parachute. So did Andy, falling fast with a closed parachute pack floating in its harness above his head. Jimmy made his way out through the rear hatch, the one in the front being still frozen, while Johnny and 'Red Berry', the navigator, were fastened to their seats in the front, and probably disabled by German bullets.

14

The fuselage landed in an almost horizontal position shockingly close to Søgaard. Its belly must almost have touched the chimneys of the building. One wing landed several hundred yards away from one of the four engines and a landing wheel. The four propellers ploughed themselves deeply into the soil.

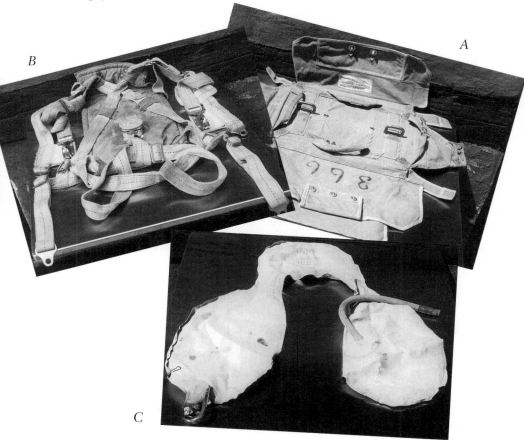

A Parachute pack, belonged to Jimmy.
Source: Holbæk Museum, photo by author.
B Parachute harness, belonged to Jimmy.
Source: Holbæk Museum, photo by author.
C Mae West, automatic inflation left, by mouth right, belonged to Jimmy.
Source: Holbæk Museum, photo by author.

A RAF heated suit. Electric wires in ducts heating back and chest and via other ducts into slippers to keep the gunner's feet warm. Sometimes he would get drowsy and switch off the heat for a minute. Quickly the gunner would turn completely cold and have to switch it on again. Belonged to Jimmy. The plate was part of the Halifax and was found at 'Hjortholmsgaarden' the day after the air duel. Source and photo: Holbæk Museum.

At this stage Jim, the rear-gunner, had already jumped from great altitude four miles away. He was as usual wearing his parachute in the tail-gun turret, which probably saved his life. He would have been unable to open the turret doors leading to the fuselage, gather his parachute from its pocket and clip the parachute on and make his escape. On the other hand, his flying boots impeded his baling out. RAF airmen wore a flying suit which incorporated electrically heated wiring which passed through the suit, down through the sleeves, trouser legs and on to the slippers. However, in order to fit the slippers into the shoes it was necessary to wear flying boots two sizes larger than normal, which meant that instead of normal size eight boots, Jim had to wear size ten. Consequently, there was little space for him to release his feet from the confines of the turret during the present emergency. Suspended or rather hanging upside down, half in – half out of the turret with one leg free, the other leg

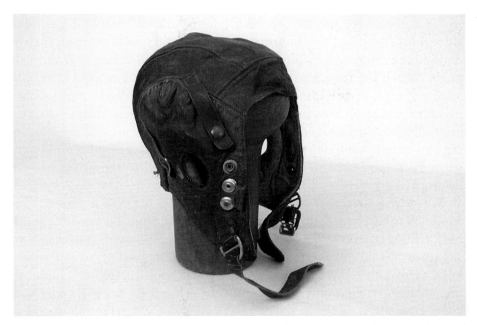

Flying helmet, leaving space for oxygen mask, and microphone. Belonged to Jimmy.
Source and photo: Holbæk Museum.

trapped in the turret, Jim took the only option available. He pulled the ripcord of his parachute hoping for the best. Fortunately, the chute literally pulled him out of the turret.

While, to his great relief, his parachute opened he found that only one clip was connected. He quickly tried to refix the second clip to his harness, but it was quite impossible and after holding it for a short while he was almost exhausted, so he had to let go and rely on the remaining clip. Now came the most unreal feeling he had ever experienced: being on the end of a parachute swinging to and fro he felt almost like hanging from a chandelier without any sense of falling. For a while he did not know whether he was dead or alive, or whether the dense cloud surrounding him was heaven or hell. His senses were restored fairly quickly, and although his Mae West had a catch for automatic inflation he decided to blow it up just to prove to himself that he was actually still alive.

Since they were yanked out at little more than a thousand feet, and since it takes the first five hundred feet for the parachute to open, the six remaining crewmembers landed close to one another. But they did not know that at the time, and they only became reunited months later, unaware of each other's fate in the meantime. Whether Berry managed to leave his seat at all is most doubtful. Johnny, the pilot, did leave the aircraft alive, but to no avail. His body bounced on the ground making an imprint clearly visible next to itself. The dead bodies of pilot and navigator both harnessed to unopened parachutes fell to the ground some distance apart.

We now know, that it was a Junker – 88G-6 D5+ZB – flown by Major Werner Husemann and wireless operator Hans-Georg Schierholz both belonging to the 1st group of *Nachtjagdgeschwader* (night fighter squadron) No. 3 of the German *Luftwaffe*. It had taken off from *Fliegerhorst Grove*, in Jutland, at 8.06 p.m. ordered to intercept and eliminate the enemy. The Germans, Husemann and Schierholz, for their part had left the air space unharmed. They were probably excited and congratulated one another on having captured yet another scalp. *Sieg Heil Indianer!* was the normal code for having shot down a 'Tommy', the joint

The body of Johnny (John Grayshan) on the field of 'Søgaard'.
Source: Holbæk Museum, photo by Christian Meldgaard

18

Junkers fighter 88G-6 similar to the aircraft flown by Husemann/ Schier-holz.
Source: Carsten Petersen, Tyske Fly i Danmark 1940-45, vol. iii, He 111 og Ju 88, Bollerup Boghandels Forlag, Ringkøbing, 1996, p.61.

designation of all-British in a uniform. Indeed, they were to add still a couple of scalps to their collection that very night.

The Junkers plane and its crew were full of fight and were soon targeting another victim. In fact, the sky was crowded with potential victims. RAF Bomber Command were attacking Chemnitz, Saxony, with no less than 717 bombers. However, we are not concerned with that huge armada here. Instead we shall focus on a smaller force entering Danish air space at the same time and sheltered by the armada. This smaller force consisted of thirty Lancaster and twenty-four Halifax bombers taking off from various British airbases at various times. Consequently, these mine-sowing aircraft were not formation flying, nor were they communicating by wireless. Their only means of contact were Morse signals by strong torches at close quarter. Wireless communication was liable to be tracked down by the enemy and direct him within range. The wireless would only be switched on for internal communication between crew members, the gunners in particular, since they were pretty isolated from their mates. Furthermore, the skipper was capable of receiving messages transmitted by his home-base, but the use of this line of communication was restricted as a last resort. As soon as the bombers had passed the line of German radar stations along the west coast of Denmark, they were certain that they had been spotted and were being pursued. They made attempts to distress enemy radar by throwing out 'window' approximately every 10th minute. There were two kinds of 'window': narrow strips of tin-foil resembling the tinsel of a Christmas tree, and the inch-wide tin-bands. Both types were intended to inflict confusion on enemy radar, which, reflecting metal objects only, was unable to distinguish between 'window' and aircraft.

The fifty-four Halifaxes and Lancasters had orders to sow their loads of mines in Stettin Bay, a sea territory code-named *Geranium*. British minefields in inner Danish waters had been coded with names of vegetables, e.g. pumpkins, asparagus, sweet pea 1-2, radish 1-2, etc., whereas waters bordering Sweden and Germany were given flower names, e.g. nasturtiums, daffodils, and geraniums. Thus the waters where the mines were sown were referred to as 'the garden'. They were dropped in parachutes from high altitude.

The German night fighters had been alerted by their air surveillance the moment the RAF bombers crossed the west coast of Denmark. Flak was fired and warnings were immediately sent to the Gedhus bunker, which was the *Zentralgefechtsstand* (centre of command) of the *Luftwaffe*. Immediately, the rather few Junker fighters based at Kastrup and Grove airfields that diminishing fuel supplies still allowed to operate, were ordered to attack. Oberleutnant Koch took off from Kastrup and soon discovered a Lancaster bomber – PB899 (QB-A) – which he hit from below setting the bomber on fire. It plunged into the sea and no crewmembers managed to bale out. Following this successful attack Koch moved west and established contact with a Halifax – MZ355 (ZL-W) – over Central Jutland. During the subsequent exchange of fire two RAF gunners, Pilot Officers Ford and Peak, were killed, whereas Squadron Leader Brittain succeeded in keeping his Halifax flying, thus enabling himself and his crew to parachute. All five, however, were taken prisoners by the *Wehrmacht*. Now, Koch turned east and over Danish waters a third Halifax – MZ924 (KN-D) – was hit. All seven flyers drowned and their bodies were washed ashore on six different islands or peninsulas.

Major Werner Husemann who was in command of 1st NJG 3 from January '44 to May '45, and his wireless operator Hans-Georg Schierholz had taken off from Grove airfield. Over Zealand they made contact with 'our' Halifax. The two RAF-gunners engaged the night fighter, which subsequently launched a counterattack. The Junkers fighter was equipped with a machine gun on top of the fuselage and was thus capable of firing obliquely and taking advantage of the blind angle of the Halifax which had no mid-gunner in a position to fire downwards. The Germans called their machine gun a *Schrägwaffen* and its volley *Schräge Musik* (German for jazz). So, Husemann manoeuvred his fighter from below and behind the English bomber into a position where the silhouette of the Halifax above against the night sky was distinct, whereas the German fighter below was almost invisible against the dark ground. From this position Schierholz aimed at the part where the wings join the body. This is where the fuel tanks are situated and where the aircraft is most vulnerable. On the other hand this part is not far from the cargo of mines and their explosion might easily pull the Junkers down with the Halifax. Husemann and Schierholz took advantage of their 'jazz'-equipment and set the Halifax ablaze from below. They, then, quickly disappeared.

Their next victim was a fourth Halifax – MZ799 (EY-X) – which burst into flames and plunged into the sea east of the island of Møn. Again there were no survivors. Six bodies were washed ashore wide apart. The Junkers fighter continued its mission but was unable to track down any more allied planes. So it landed at Stade airfield just west of Hamburg. This was their 250th flight as a team, and thus they were celebrating a successful jubilee. Schierholz (age 23) who had been shot down himself four times and had been severely wounded in action three months earlier when he and Husemann had crash-landed near Herning,

Major Werner Husemann's Gruppe. A Geschwader consisted of 100-160 aircraft, divided into 3-4 Gruppen (indicated in Roman numerals) each of approximately 30-40 aircraft. In turn each Gruppe was made up of 3 Staffeln (indicated in Arabic numerals), these having 12-16 aircraft. Werner Husemann sitting at the middle of the lower row, Oberleutnant Koch No. 2 from the right in the middle row. The photograph was taken at Fliegerhorst Grove medio April '45, a couple of weeks before the German capitulation. Source: private archive

was decorated with the Knight's Cross for his fifty-seven direct hits. So was major Husemann (age 25) who was credited with having shot down a total of forty RAF bombers.

When the crewmembers of the Halifax MZ793 (ZA-X) were gliding through the air in their parachutes they had very little time to reflect on the fact that they were approaching hostile territory. Denmark like most other countries in Europe was occupied by Nazi-Germany. Before August '43 the Danish police force was still maintaining law and order and had generally obeyed orders given by the collaborating government and handed over allied air crews to the *Wehrmacht*... The Danish Cabinet ceased collaborating – at least formally – and resigned in August '43, and in September '44 the police had been rounded up and disarmed by the Germans – and 2000 constables sent to concentration camps in Germany. Others went underground at home to join the Resistance movement. Thus prospects now were somewhat brighter for allied airmen forced to bale out or land here. There were, however, still about 180,000 German troops in the country. Governmental authorities as well as the population were divided as regards loyalty towards the rule of law inside the framework of collaboration and the courage to perform acts of civil disobedience.

So, on this February night in 1945 a crew of shocked RAF airmen drifting in their parachutes anticipated landing in a territory where they were likely to confront their martial enemy, but might stumble on a well wisher. Danish citizens hiding or clothing allied airmen let alone helping them to escape were liable to be at least arrested and at worst to face a German firing squad. In August '42 the Ministry of Justice had instructed the Danish Police to arrest all members of allied aircrews upon their landing here and hand them over at once to the German *Wehrmacht*. An impression of the particular attitude of Danish authorities in this respect is given by a circular of 24th December, '42 from the State Prosecutor requiring Chief Constables in all cities with a hospital to convey to the medical staff: demonstrations of sympathy by Danes towards allied patients in the form of letters or flowers were not to be allowed!

People of the Søby-region where the Halifax had happened to crash lived as smallholders in a close community. Their plots had been parcelled out in the 1920ies from Søgaard, a former manor turned into an old peoples' home. These farming families oscillated between nervousness at breaking the curfew and curiosity to find out if there was something to appropriate. Here as all over Europe scarcity and rationing of goods prevailed. So, the locals did not go out to gather relics; what they were after were useful materials like pieces of plexi-glass for repairs, scraps of metal, copper wires that could be melted and sold for ten kroner each kilogram, rubber tyres for soles, parachutes for dresses, almost anything of value. Some helpings of Horlicks, a palatable stimulant, on board the Halifax, in ways past finding out ended up with some pupils at Stenhus Kostskole, in Holbæk. They indulged these delights while

Rear-tail turret and machine-guns (Browning) from Halifax MZ793 (ZA-X) landed north of Søgaard. The weapons were falsely claimed to have been handed over to the Resistance. Source: Holbæk Museum, photo by Christian Meldgaard.

Mid-upper turret landed on the east side of Søgaard, opposite the fuselage. Source: Holbæk Museum, photo by Christian Meldgaard.

sweating over their written assignments that summer for the benefit of their higher certificate marks.

A certain carrier from Holbæk claimed to have managed to appropriate two machine guns and a box of ammunition from the Halifax. After having cleaned the weapons he claimed to have delivered them to the Resistance movement, of which he wasn't an active member himself, in exchange for a revolver. The case was brought up after war, when the police charged him with illegal possession of this revolver. The suspect had a witness summoned who supported his statement, but two witnesses from the Resistance denied having received anything from him except one stolen German hand granade.

While the Danes snatched what they could get at, the Germans a few days later carried the fuselage and wings of the Halifax away on a truck. They also exploded one of the mines causing damage to more window panes and tiles of neighbouring buildings let alone leaving a fissure in a

One of the four mines ploughing itself into the field. Exploded by the Germans.
Source: Holbæk Museum, photo by Christian Meldgaard.

25

medieval vault of Sønder Asmindrup Church some six hundred yards away. Local rumours have it that another unexploded mine is still on the bottom of the pond of Søgaard.

THE RAF CREW

Who were they these seven members of the aircrew of Halifax ZA-X from RAF 10 Squadron? How were they recruited? What were their occupations in civilian life? And how did they perceive fighting against Nazi-Germany?

The crew of Halifax Mk. B.III MZ793 (ZA-X), RAF 10 Squadron home-based at Melbourne, Yorkshire. The persons are from left to right: 'Red Berry', Andy, Johnny, Jim and Jimmy. The photograph was taken September '44, when the crew was formed and trained on a Wellington aircraft at Lossiemouth, Scotland. Later-on Stan and Roy joined the crew.
Source: private archive

Johnny	187810 F/O John Grayshan, pilot, RAF (VR), 23, married
'Red' Berry	1800664 F/Sgt. Alfred James Berry, navigator, RAF (VR), 22
Stan	187883 P/O Stanley Chaderton, bomb aimer, RAF, 22
Andy	1811552 F/Sgt. Peter Frederick Andrews, wireless operator, RAF, 20
Roy	2205669 Sgt. Roy Maddock-Lyon, flight engineer, RAF, 20
Jimmy	1579147 F/Sgt. Horace L. Mills, mid-upper gunner, RAF, 23, married
Jim	1090310 F/Sgt. James Petre, rear-gunner, RAF, 24, married

F/O Flying Officer, F/S Flight Sergeant, P/O Pilot Officer, VR Volunteer Reserve

RAF flying crews only recruited volunteers. The crewmembers might also have volunteered for the submarines or for the airborne forces. Johnny Grayshan, the son of a Lancashire working class family, volunteered for the RAF at 18. He had done well at school and the high marks of his higher school certificate gained him a grant to enter the university. But the outbreak of the war put an end to all that. In '39 he went with the first company of British cadets to be trained in the United States where he received the Silver Wings of the USAF before sailing back to the UK. He started his duties as an RAF flying instructor for eighteen months at Lossiemouth airbase, Scotland, where he trained his crew of five on a Wellington. Finally, he became captain of the Halifax at which time Roy and Stan joined the crew.

Other crewmembers had joined the RAF during '42, one of them in '43. Jim had also been trained in the US to become a pilot and he and Johnny got acquainted there. Jim, however, failed to pass the final test as a pilot and did not make a second go at it. Back in the UK crews were formed at Lossiemouth and Johnny asked Jim to join his crew, which he gladly did. He used to be a construction engineer. Roy held a higher national certificate of mechanical engineering after four years' apprenticeship and night school. Alternatively, he could have continued his studies or he could have become a teacher. Education was considered beneficial to the country in wartime, too. Jimmy was a transport driver in London, and Stan had been a dockworker in Liverpool. Andy had signed a contract with the Air Training Corporation when he was only seventeen, i.e. before he had entered an apprenticeship in upholstery.

Four of the seven crewmembers were bachelors, but Johnny and Jim had married in '42 and were by now fathers of two and three children respectively, while Jimmy's wife was expecting their first baby.

By early '36 it had become obvious that Nazi Germany was rearming at a a furious pace and had the will to use its power in war if necessary. In depression-torn England, the RAF finally persuaded the Air Ministry and the Government that it was going to have to expand its strength greatly to meet the threat. Among the results of these deliberations was the order to Handley Page to design a bomber. The first prototype proved to be underpowered, so a second prototype was equipped with four Bristol Hercules radial engines and the new Mk III version showed a dramatic increase in performance. At its official christening by Lord Halifax, in September '41, he quoted a old Yorkshire prayer: *From Hull, Hell and Halifax, good Lord, deliver us!*. And so it turned out to be. Production built up rapidly, thanks to the Handley Page split-unit design, and the Halifax Mk III became the right arm of Bomber Command together with the Avro Lancaster B.III. A total of 6,176 Halifax's were built, and they carried out no less than 82,000 operational sorties, dropping almost 250,000 tons of bombs. The Halifax MZ 793 (ZA-X), which is in focus here, was built at Speke, Liverpool.

By February '45 these seven airmen had already been a crew for some time and knew each other well. The were all very close. Besides operating the wireless and radar it was also part of Andy's duties to drop 'window', and Roy was responsible for the fuel supply, engines and the aircraft function ability as well as dropping the two types of 'window' already mentioned. In October '44 they had taken part in a heavy raid on Essen in a force of 1055 bombers, which devastated part of the Krupp works. Less than ten bombers failed to return to base.

The crew were not particularly concerned with the German extinction camps, of which they knew very little at that time. Nor were they preoccupied with the ideology of Nazism. What motivated them to volunteer was rather a sense of patriotism, a conviction that Hitler was evil, and that Britain and the entire Empire was threatened with extinction. They found Chamberlain's policy of appeasement defeatist and futile and were prepared to follow Churchill whose firm stand against Hitler during the Battle of Britain relied totally on the RAF 'lads'. Flying was not a matter of politics. Even appeasers had become fighters. After the Soviet Union and the USA had joined Britain as allies, victory was a matter of time although there was yet immense individual suffering to be endured.

The crew did not simply consider the bombing of Germany an act of revenge. In the Battle of Britain, Spitfires and Hurricanes of the Fighter Command had engaged German bombers, and Bomber Command had forced the German runways in occupied France to be laid further and further south. In the beginning of the war the Germans nearly got the upper hand and coined a new word *coventrieren* (after the damage done to the city of Coventry). After the allied invasion of France the roles were reversed. Allied armadas were carpet-bombing German industrial plants and cities, and German fighters tried to disable a maximum of allied bombers. At this point the air war was a professional affair based on technology, skill and industrial capacity.

To Air-Marshall Arthur Harris, head of Bomber Command, the British strategy was based on cool, economic calculation. The enemy's costs related to the dropping of one ton of bombs on Britain was calculated at 20,500 man-hours, equal to the costs of building a Lancaster. The point was, that every single Lancaster returning unharmed after having aimed its load of bombs at German armament factories could be regarded as fully written off. Every successive mission could be considered a pure net gain. The aces of the Luftwaffe attracted a great deal of hero-worship particularly towards the end of the war, when a shortage of fuel became a constraint to the German air war effort. The experience and skill of the individual fighter pilots became significant factors when it had to be decided who should intercept enemy aircraft and how often. The RAF, too, of course decorated their bravest and most efficient pilots with medals. The ideological justification of warfare was only emphasized in hindsight, when the atrocities committed in concentration camps were mass communicated. However, at the time, the priorities of the Halifax-crew were different, and they were not familiar with the cool calculations of 'Bomber-Harris'. Their main concern was to stay alive and to see their mates safely home after an air raid over hostile territory. The chances of returning alive had improved lately because the lack of fuel kept the *Nachtjagd-geschwader* on the ground. The day before the crash, an armada of RAF bombers with a loss of only 1.2 per cent had devastated defenceless Dresden.

The mission of 14th February, however, was to be their last mission as a team. Roy mentions that on this day he had a hunch that he would be shot down. He had asked his closest friend at the time, Harold, to accompany him to the railway station on Roy's return from home leave. Roy told Harold of his premonition. This was echoed in flight by Jimmy, one of the gunners, who tested the machine guns by firing into the water. 'Why do you do that?' Roy asked. 'We always do that', Jimmy replied. 'No, at least you never told us before that you wanted to test the machine guns', Roy commented nervously.

As already mentioned, the goal of this mission was to sow four mines in the Bay of Stettin. The crew believed that the mining of *Geranium* would prevent the first German aircraft carrier from leaving the dockyards at Stettin and thence to the Baltic and the Atlantic to bring havoc to allied operations wherever possible. At least this was what the crew was briefed to think by Bomber Command. However, no German aircraft carrier made it through the minefield, for the simple reason that no such vessel was ever built. From January '43 the *Seekriegsleitung* had abandoned all plans to build heavy high sea battleships never mind aircraft carriers. Quite the opposite: The German Navy was applying a strategy of continued submarine warfare and enhanced coastal defence artillery for which they needed all the steel and manpower available. Consequently, the Navy planned to scrap large men-of-war and remelt the steel for shore batteries. Air protection of shore batteries could be more readily provided from airfields on the ground than on ships, and besides it was doubtful that the *Luftwaffe* was prepared to divert their forces to naval vessels. Before the outbreak of the war, however, there had been plans to build aircraft carriers, but the engines produced for this purpose were transferred to battle cruisers.

However, the airmen were not only briefed about their mission of sowing their load of four heavy mines (2,000 lbs. each), two acoustic and two magnetic. They were also provided with an RAF escape kit.

Nicknamed a 'Pandora' for its precious contents, it consisted of a silk map, Danish and German currency, a compass, a fishing line & hook, a lighter, a whistle, a pouch of luminescent powder to notify allied aircraft, morphine and burn bandages, chocolate, and Horlicks tablets for energy. Finally, they were told what to do in the event of being unlucky enough to have to bale out or forced to land behind the enemy's lines.

A. It is everybody's duty to evade capture or to escape and to rejoin their units.

B. If for any reason you are unable to evade capture, then you still have a duty to your country. That is to deny to the other side information which he badly needs.

C. There is no doubt that an enormous amount of information is obtained from POWs and much time and trouble is spent by the enemy in obtaining this

D. As members of the RAF you are particularly prized as sources of information, although in the past the RAF have been extremely security-minded.

Do not imagine, however, that direct questioning is the only method the other side employs to obtain the information he wants. If you are unlucky enough to be taken prisoner the Germans are likely to invite you into the mess where you are given food and drink and an air of friendliness prevails. But you will find that the amount of drink consumed will loosen your tongue. A few indirect questions put by the interrogation officer leads you to say things you would much prefer to keep quiet about. And it is a shaking experience to find that the interrogations officer asks you how so-and-so is of your own particular squadron, or says that last week so-and-so was taken POW. The natural reaction to this is 'Well, if he knows all about us, why should I worry to be careful?' But you must realize that it is only because

others have talked, or have carried documents with them against orde
that such records can be built up. Quite apart from direct questioning
there are many other methods employed in order to obtain information:
stool pigeon etc... Therefore be always on your guard and give nothing
but rank, name and number.

Source: M.R.D. Foot and J.M. Langley, MI-9. Escape and Evasion, 1939-45, London, 1979.

~RSDAY 15TH – DAY TWO

Thursday morning each family of the forlorn crew had been informed by telegram that their son or husband had failed to return last night. This could be taken to mean either that he had been killed in action or that he had been taken POW. This was a bad omen likely to induce fathers and mothers, wives and girlfriends to despair.

TWO DECEASED AIRMEN

Two crewmembers probably never regained consciousness after they were flung out of the splintered aircraft. Johnny, the pilot, a husband and father of two children, was found the next morning on the field. He lay there with his parachute pack as closed as when Roy had clicked it on for him. Rev. With Johannesen wrote a letter to the widow immediately after the war, comforting her that her husband's face pointing towards the sky had showed no signs of suffering. Another eyewitness describes two bullet-holes in his body and bloodstains inside the fuselage of the Halifax. Both pieces of evidence make it probable that German bullets hit the pilot when they attacked the second time.

Christian Meldgaard, a professional photographer and a committed member of the Resistance movement, took a photograph of his body. In the open Christian worked as a press photographer for 'Holbæk Amtstidende', a local newspaper, together with Adolph Rastén, a Jew and a well known post-war foreign correspondent; sheltered by this legal activity Christian also carried out photographic work for the Resistance such as developing and copying negatives of German defence lines along the west coast of Jutland and providing propaganda material for the illegal press. Returning pictures of the sabotage of 'Rimas', Ringsted Machine Works, to a post office box for the local underground, he was

34

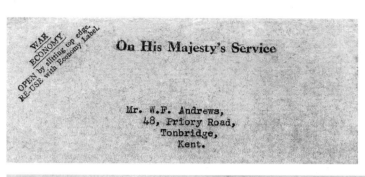

On His Majesty's Service

WAR ECONOMY
OPEN by slitting top edge.
RE-USE with Economy Label.

Mr. W.F. Andrews,
48, Priory Road,
Tonbridge,
Kent.

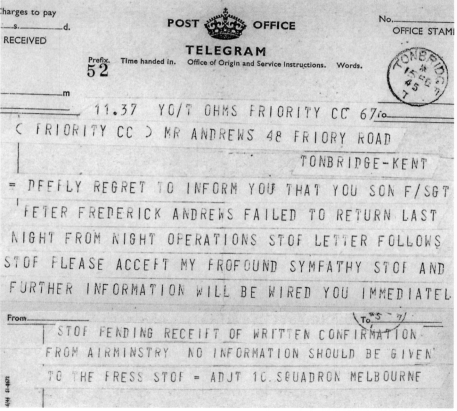

Charges to pay

—s.——d.

RECEIVED

——m

POST OFFICE

TELEGRAM

Prefix. **52** Time handed in. Office of Origin and Service Instructions. Words.

No.———

OFFICE STAMP

11.37 YO/T OHMS FRIORITY CC 67io

(FRIORITY CC) MR ANDREWS 48 FRIORY ROAD

TONBRIDGE-KENT

= DEEFLY REGRET TO INFORM YOU THAT YOU SON F/SGT
FETER FREDERICK ANDREWS FAILED TO RETURN LAST
NIGHT FROM NIGHT OPERATIONS STOF LETTER FOLLOWS
STOF FLEASE ACCEFT MY FROFOUND SYMFATHY STOF AND
FURTHER INFORMATION WILL BE WIRED YOU IMMEDIATEL

From———

To #5 - 7/

STOF FENDING RECEIFT OF WRITTEN CONFIRMATION
FROM AIRMINSTRY   NO INFORMATION SHOULD BE GIVEN
TO THE FRESS STOF = ADJT 1C. SQUADRON MELBOURNE

Telegram of 15th February, '45 from 10 Squadron, Melbourne, to Mr. W.F. Andrews, Tonbridge, to the effect that Andy had failed to return last night. Source: private archive.

Fuselage seen from the end.
Source: Holbæk Museum, photo by Christian Meldgaard.

careless enough to send his compliments, and when the Germans snatched the parcel, Christian was arrested and imprisoned at Vestre Fængsel, prison cell 233, where he was cruelly tortured. The Germans, however, were unable to make him yield evidence of his illegal activities, and when a month later in October '43 they needed room for Jews and their helpers under arrest, Christian was released in a condition of permanent injury.

After his imprisonment he resumed his double life, working for the Danish and German authorities while at the same time forging papers for the underground and a few German deserters. In May '44 the Germans ordered all citizens to carry papers of identification issued by the local authorities. Christian was overloaded with work and as a consequence was given legal access to the films, photographic chemicals and

Christian & Minna Meldgaard, Holbæk, photographers and freedom-fighters, reunited with their children at Christmas '45. Brita is sitting with her doll on the lap of her godmother.
Source: private archive.

paper he so badly needed for his illegal activities. The German jamming station at Sandbakkevej, Vipperød, impeding Danes from listening to the BBC news, was an important local target of sabotage. This was photographed in great detail from the outside as well as from the inside by

Christian prior to its being completely devastated on New Year's Eve '44-'45 by a local sabotage group.

Christian's wife, Minna, was a professional photographer, too, and together they issued plenty of illegal documents assisted by Warrant Officer, P.K. Jensen, who had a mania for official stamps from all over the country. In September '44 when the German forces swooped on all police stations, many of those who were incidentally off duty and hence not arrested went underground and badly needed false papers. By presenting the proper code word they were issued with identity papers stating the most peculiar places of birth and professions. Hence Christian was periodically forced to go underground, and was sheltered for at a time at Havremarken, in Jens Peter Petersen's house, Johannes Helms's neighbour, and in Rev. Johannesen's vicarage less than a mile from the wreck of the Halifax.

On the morning of the 15th February he was ordered by the Wehrmacht (since August '43 occupying Holbæk Barracks) to cover the crash of the Halifax bomber. He had a number of skills useful for the job. His

German Feldwebel (Military Police) patrol watching Johnny's body near Søgaard. Note the white spot in the middle rear, which is Roy's parachute. Also note the tower at Sønder Asmindrup Church to the right top.
Source: Holbæk Museum, photo by Christian Meldgaard.

38

German was good. He was adamant and he never took a 'no' for an answer. So, armed with his camera he approached the site guarded by twelve German *Feldwebel* who denied him access despite his claim that he was working on German orders. Christian, however, insisted that either the *Feldwebel* gave him permission to take the pictures he had been ordered to take or he would call upon their Superior Officer, Hauptmann so and so, office room No. so and so. Finally, confronted by this menace, the German patrol gave in and a series of unique photographs were taken. One of them shows the deceased John Grayshan.

'Red' Berry, the navigator, a bachelor aged 22, had landed face downwards also very close to the wreck. If he left the blazing cage at all it was in the last seconds only. He, too, was killed on the threshold of his adult

The fuselage of the Halifax, close to 'Søgaard'. In front of the fuselage some unknown Dane wearing a RAF leather jacket and flying helmet. These must have belonged to 'Red' Berry.
Source: Holbæk Museum, photo by Christian Meldgaard.

life in a state of unconsciousness, his face looking calm. His body was found before midnight and taken away to the hospital at Holbæk. A photograph taken by Christian the following day shows an unknown person wearing a RAF leather jacket and flying helmet. 'Red' Berry was the only member of crew wearing this type of leather jacket, so it must have been stolen from his dead body.

The Germans collected the bodies at Holbæk Hospital the next day and buried them immediately without ceremony. No doctor was called to examine the corpses and to issue medical clearance certificates. It is hard to explain why no ceremony was arranged. Previously, on 27th January '43, when Mosquito DZ407 (GB-R) from 105 Squadron had crashed at Tveje Merløse as it returned from bombing Burmeister &

Several German Feldwebel leaving the burial ceremony of J.G. Cox and R.H. Dawson at Tveje Merløse Churchyard shortly after 29th January '43. Source: private archive, photo by Christian Meldgaard

Wain, the large shipyard in Copenhagen working for the Germans, the two RAF airmen, Cox and Dawson, had been honourably buried by the Germans. For propaganda purposes Christian had been ordered to take photographs of the stately coffins, the ostentatious flowers and in particular the last salute of honour fired by the green squad. By February '45 proper ceremonial formalities had been abandoned.

TWO INJURED AIRMEN

Andy, the wireless operator, woke up as he was falling fast to see clouds streaming past only to realise that his parachute pack was floating above his head while still clicked unto his harness. He reached up and pulled the release handle, felt a sharp jerk and shortly afterwards he landed in a muddy field. The parachute harness had badly bruised the lower part of his body. He saw carbide lamps swinging in the distance and was making his way towards them when he came across a small group of houses. He indicated to the people that he was with the RAF and they directed him towards a house belonging to the Møller family. Andy assumed he would get help there so he knocked on a lighted window. However, the door remained closed; it was then Andy realised that his hands were badly lacerated. The family was scared and did not know what to do. So they did nothing. The next morning when Mr. Møller saw the bloodstains on his doorstep and learned about their origin he felt ashamed. Andy walked on to the next farmhouse, owned by Theodor Jeppesen (all smallholdings in a row) where he was taken in and given first aid. He had no clue where he was, so he took out his escape kit, unfolded his silk map, and asked his helpers to show him where he was.

Stan, the bomb aimer, does not recall the seconds immediately after the explosion. But he does remember clearly that he was falling fast through space. As in Andy's case, Stan's parachute had gone from his chest to over his head. He reached out for the ripcord, pulled it, and floated down to earth, landing in a field at some distance from Andy. He released the parachute, hid it at the edge of the field, and started walking towards a barn not far from a cluster of houses. He sat down in this

A

B

C

A Propeller from one of the four engines of the Halifax ploughed into the soil.
Source: private archive, photo by Christian Meldgaard.
B A landing wheel from the Halifax. In the background smallholders' farms at Søby.
Source: The Resistance Museum, Copenhagen, photo by Christian Meldgaard.
C Parts of Halifax wreckage collected and placed on Skovvejen next to the avenue, leading to the old people's home at 'Søgaard'. In the background Theodor Jeppesen's house, where Andy was offered some comfort.
Source: The Resistance Museum, Copenhagen, photo by Christian Meldgaard.

D

D Children playing on wing. Skovvejen in the background.
Source: private archive, photo by Christian Meldgaard.

barn feeling sorry for himself, his ribs ached and blood was flowing down his face from a gash on his forehead. Then a light went on in the nearest house and a lady started washing up. Being in pain he plucked up courage, went over to the house and asked for help. The lady was shocked to see this stranger, but took him to Doctor Vilhelm Schlippe's house in Sønder Jernløse, the next village. The doctor's wife who spoke English cleaned him up and gave him a drink. Then she sent for an ambulance judging that Stan was in need of hospital treatment.

Andy remembers that after half an hour an ambulance arrived at Jeppesen's place. Esther, the daughter of the house, patted his cheek for at good-bye, and he was assisted into the vehicle, which had probably arrived on the initiative of the salvage corps in Holbæk. The ambulance stopped after a short distance, the back doors opened, and in came Stan looking very much the worse for wear. At Holbæk Hospital Andy and Stan lay side by side and were treated by various nurses and a doctor who could speak English. Stan needed treatment for his damaged ribs, the gash on his head and another one on his back. Andy was less hurt. The nurses told them that the Germans were looking for them but that they would try to hide them and pass them on to the underground movement. The doctor introduced them to two members of the Resistance who said that they would evacuate them the following day, if they were fit enough to travel. In the meantime they were moved from ward to ward by nurses to prevent them from getting caught.

Stan and Andy spent the 15th at the hospital. The moving of the airmen stirred up a lot of anxiety. Would the Resistance people arrange for their escape as promised? There wasn't much Andy and Stan could do to influence the course of events. At any rate they were receiving medical aid and as to their predicament they could only hope for the best.

THREE ESCAPEES

Roy, too, was unconscious as he glided from heaven to earth. In his dreaming state of mind he was in his room at home chatting to his younger brother. Suddenly, a violent pull from the parachute made him return to reality. He had lost his flying boots, his flying helmet, and his gloves, and one of his thumbs was swollen. Unbeknown to him Roy had landed only a hundred metres from his pilot. It was bitterly cold although not frosty and his bare feet made his footprints in the six-inch layer of mud dangerously conspicuous to hostile pursuers. His premonition from his chat with Harold had come true and he was in deep shock.

At the last briefing the crew had been advised to make contact with local clergymen or doctors in the event that they were shot down over occupied Denmark. Flemming Juncker, leader of SOE's dropping opera-

F/Sgt. Roy Maddock-Lyon (age 20)
Source: private archive.

tions in Denmark, was the source of this advice and the Danish Resistance Movement had established a secret network and a code enabling adepts to provide for the safety and rescue of allied airmen. But how was Roy to find the nearest vicarage situated, as he was on a pitch dark winter night in the middle of nowhere? Another piece of advice slumbered in his mind: never to ask for help at the nearest farmhouse, since this will be the most obvious place for the enemy to look for you. So walk further away from your landing spot and don't leave your parachute or any other 'visiting card' like a Mae West or a parachute harness. Conspicuous in his British uniform Roy was desperate. He was aware that the first twenty-four hours were decisive. 'If I survive that long my chances of embarking on an evasion will be good. But will I run into a friend or a foe in this quasi-hostile country that was known to behave as ambivalently as Hamlet, its former Prince? 'To be, or not to be, – that is the question.'

Pondering on the advice he had been given it struck him that he was carrying 'a Pandora'. Under the circumstances these items seemed to be of little avail. When he was unaware of his position what was the use of a compass direction? Which procedure would guide him to the nearest priest or doctor, whose services he needed more badly than ever?

His footprints led to a road about 150 yards away. Following that road he arrived at a farm house and got eye-contact with a little girl standing outside and watching from a distance the fading flames of the wrecked Halifax. This house was too close. Roy decided to walk on as he realised that his footprints might reveal him anyway. He discovered that he was being followed by somebody and pointing at the burning aircraft he cried, 'Shot down, bom-bom, shot down, bom-bom. Help me! Do something!' A man opened a gate and led Roy into the farmhouse, where his wife and daughter were waiting. The daughter was the little girl he had first met. Ingrid was her name. The man was Ejner Næsholt Sørensen, a smallholder. His wife was terrified. None of them spoke any English. What would happen to the family once the Germans searched their house and found the foreigner? Yet, the wretched flyer was washed and fed, escorted upstairs and put to bed.

The next morning Ingrid entered his room. The temperature had sunk

Ejner Næsholt Sørensen's small-holding farm, Skov-vejen, Søby.
Source: private archive.

Ejner Næsholt Sø-rensen and family. Ingrid in the middle.
Source: private archive.

and the window panes were covered by ice ferns being the frozen damp of Roy's breath. Ingrid started rubbing the pane to enable Roy to take a look outside through the leafless trees. 'No, no! Then they may see us.' Outside a German patrol of a dozen *Feldwebel* was searching the terrain around the wreck. Then he saw some ambulance people carry a body away from the field on a stretcher. The lifeless body was covered, so he could not see Johnny's face. It struck him that he was left in complete ignorance of the fate of his comrades. All he did know now was that at least one had died.

On the road in the opposite direction the milkman from Kvanløse Co-operative Dairy was loading cans, and Ejner was exchanging words with him. As the milkman was driving his horse and cart away, Ejner entered Roy's room to tell him in halting English that he would be picked up by the milkman the same evening after dark. What Roy did not know and what the smallholder could not explain was that this milkman was an extraordinary one, a man of education and experience, and fluent in English after having spent his shabby youth in the United States. His friends and family called Johannes Helms, with whom we are already acquainted, since the evening before he had been on the lookout for survivors, Hanse. Ejner had guessed that Hanse belonged to the Resistance as indeed he did. He was helping to collect and drive away containers of weapons dropped by the SOE in Brorfelde Forest a few miles away. Ejner was worried about the reactions of his panic-stricken wife and had briefed Hanse who promised to fetch the Englishman at dusk. Hanse regretted that he had not been informed in time to have the two injured flyers transported to Kalundborg Hospital which was in the hands of doctors loyal to the Resistance rather than to Holbæk which was considered less safe. As to the endangered airman upstairs he ought to be transferred to the hayloft for the meantime. Roy had been trained to know that if hiding under hay one should make sure to cover oneself by a considerable layer, since a hostile bayonet is likely to penetrate very deeply. German patrols continued searching farmhouses during the afternoon.

Hanse came to pick up Roy at six o'clock bringing a pair of boots several sizes too big. Under cover of darkness they crossed together the fields towards Hanse's farmhouse at Havremarken luckily avoiding the German patrols on the alert. Ejner, still very uneasy about the danger in which he was mixed up took another precautionary measure: He followed Hanse's footsteps one by one to and fro in order to prevent an imaginary dog of a German patrol to retrieve the scent of Roy. In his mind he had already made up a story that he had been taking a stroll should he be exposed to a grilling.

Roy was now installed in the loft of Hanse's farmhouse, which was only used as dry storage place for the annual harvest of barley. In fact, Roy was hidden right here in the room – now my study – where this narrative is being written. In 1975, when as a prospective buyer I came to see Hanse's place for the first time, I noticed a diploma on the wall signed by General Dwight D.Eisenhower. This spurred a lively and fascinating story, which it seemed to me deserved to be written down for the public. In this room, a bed was now set up for Roy and Mrs. Rigborg Helms began adjusting one of her husband's suits to fit the much shorter flyer. He must resemble an ordinary Dane.

Immediately after his talk with Ejner, Hanse stopped at a small grocer's shop on the corner to arrange yet another transfer for Roy, this time to Copenhagen. His brother-in-law, Dr. Carl Syrach-Larsen married to Hanse's sister Nina, was a forest botanist and head of an arboretum in Charlottenlund, some eight miles north of Copenhagen. Carl had been travelling a lot collecting shrubs and trees from all parts of the world and he had also presented the Helms family with some exotic species still embellishing my garden at Havremarken. The two families spent much time together, e.g. for the summer of '44 the Syrach-Larsen family had rented the neighbour's house in Havremarken, i.e. Jens Peter Petersen's place where Christian Meldgaard had been staying underground. Like Hanse, Carl was involved in Resistance work.

Aware that telephone conversations might be tapped, Hanse borrowed the grocer's phone to inform Carl that he and Rigborg were being paid a visit from a friend of Bodil, his second sister, and he asked Carl in passing if he had heard the news about an English aircraft having crashed in the neighbourhood? As a matter of fact Hanse's and Nina's sister, Bodil, was married to an Englishman and living in Britain, and due to the war she was unable to communicate with her relatives in Denmark except for vapid remarks exchanged via the Red Cross. 'I'm delighted to hear this and would very much like to meet him.' Carl replied and continued, 'Yes, we heard about the crash. Could you both come and see us to-morrow?'

Having been initiated to the scheme Roy's shock eased off into some sort of bewildered hope. During his first twenty-four hours in occupied territory he had happened to meet this English-speaking smallholder who seemed helpful enough. But could he be trusted? Hanse had even been attentive enough to go and pick up Roy's parachute and harness so as to eliminate the two most revealing clues.

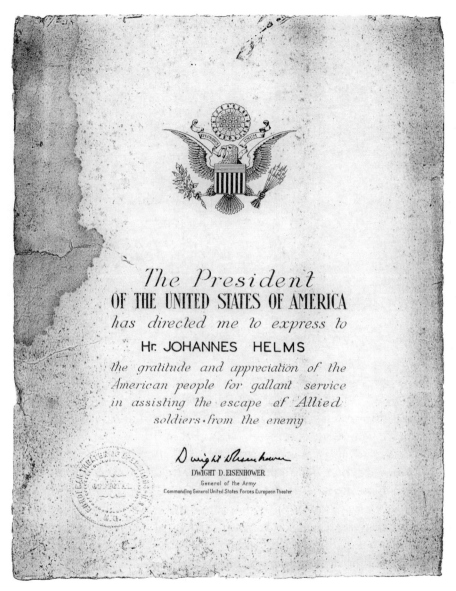

Diploma from Shaef Commander, General Dwight D. Eisenhower to Johannes Helms, Havremarken.
Source: private archive.

The Helms family, summer '44 (Rigborg and Hanse, Niels Ebbe, Agnete, and Peter Andreas)
Source: private archive.

* * * * *

Jimmy, the mid-upper gunner, had been forced to land in a small tree, not far away from Roy, completely wrapped in his own parachute. One of the curious locals, a young farm labourer, showed up to snatch the precious material of the parachute and had already started folding it up, when suddenly a man came out of the other end. Jimmy was still wearing it! Presumably the young Dane quickly removed himself from the scene. Jimmy then spent some time getting rid of his parachute, life jacket and other equipment by hiding it in a thicket. Subsequently, he moved in another direction towards Sønder Asmindrup where he ran into Karl Petersen's wife, Vera. Karl himself, the village blacksmith, had been alerted by the explosion and had walked out to see what was happening. Seeing Jimmy he took him into his house. Jimmy suspected he had landed in Sweden and asked Karl, who speaking very little English shook his head. Jimmy then asked if he was in Germany? Unable to make himself understood he raised his arm shouting *'Heil Hitler?'*. 'No, no', was the answer, 'Danmark!' Karl lived close to the parish clergyman, Rev. Paul With Johannesen, whom Jimmy later-on congratulated by calling him a wizard at English. Paul now introduced himself and told Jimmy that he had been out looking for the crew. This reminded the air gunner of what he had been told at the briefing before take-off from Melbourne. So, unawares he had been sluiced into the first link of an escape network. But would it work?

It was agreed that Karl was to put up Jimmy for the night in his work-

Jimmy's RAF identity card F/Sgt. Horace Leslie Mills No.1025337 issued July '44.
Source: private archive

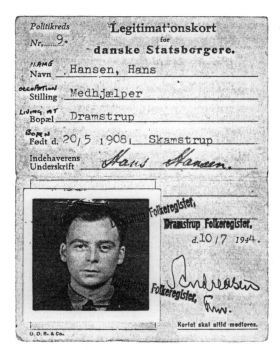

shop. Early in the morning Esther, the vicar's wife went by bicycle to Holbæk to contact P.K. Jensen and Christian Meldgaard's wife, Minna. P.K. was an army officer who had been serving at the Barracks of Holbæk, but went underground after August '43 when the Germans seized the barracks and its store of weapons. He was the local head of an important Resistance group, *Ringen* ('The Ring', a national Resistance group grown out of a study circle) and at the same time he was also in charge of the local committee of *Danmarks Frihedsråd* (The Freedom Council of Denmark) which struggled underground to assert itself as an alternative to Cabinet authority. P.K. was an avid collector of stamps from authorities from all over the country: He made copies of those stamps, and Christian and Minna had a drawer at their photo-shop containing blank identity papers.

Esther returned to Sønder Asmindrup bringing with her a stamped but otherwise blank identity card which enabled them to provide Jimmy with an authorized document transforming the RAF Flight Sergeant No. 1579147 into Mr. Hans Hansen, a farm worker living at Dramstrup. He now rehearsed the pronunciation of his new name with some conviction. As already mentioned, Christian was living underground at the vicarage during this period. His help was not needed, though, because Jimmy had the required photograph of himself in his escape-kit.

On 11th March, nearly a month later Christian was recognized by the very same *Obergefreiter*, who had found Christian's behaviour at 'Søgaard' suspicious when 'coincidentally' this time, too, out of nowhere, Christian was on the spot taking snapshots when the fuel stores of DDPA (Det Danske Petroleums Aktieselskab, 'Danish Petroleum Ltd.') at Holbæk Harbour were set ablaze by a local sabotage group. So, that evening Christian was notified by one of his young helpers from his orienteering club that Ib Birkedal Hansen, 'King of Informers' with his own office at Shellhuset, and his gang of Hipos were on their way to arrest him at No. 13, Ahlgade, where he had his photo-shop and flat. Christian climbed onto the roof and escaped across the roofs of adjacent buildings. Brita, his five year old daughter and the last child of three still at home, the two others being looked after elsewhere by friends, remembers how the Hipo-minions searched the shop, emptied drawers and pushed everything down from the shelves as she turned against them and ordered them to stop. Minna with her hands up for several hours cried, but her little girl warned the soldiers not to open the next drawer because that was where she kept her toys. Nobody present but Minna knew that the next drawer contained their stock of identity papers. Unexpectedly, the Danish minions obeyed the child.

The young fellow from the orienteering club went around to sound out the police station, at that time the Gestapo headquarters at Holbæk, and reported to Christian that his wife and daughter would be taken hostages by Birkedal the following evening to force him to surface, so immediately the family cycled to the island of Møn where they found temporary shelter in the house of Christian's mother. Many times in the months to come Christian and Minna themselves were in need of their expertise at swopping identities. By the way, Birkedal had forgotten his Borsalino, a trilby hat, in the photo-shop, and Minna often wore it in triumph after the liberation. Birkedal and his gang of traitors were the most brutal terrorists during the war and he was sentenced to death in 1950 as part of the post war judicial settlement.

The next morning Jimmy was told that if the Germans showed up he was to hide behind some bales of straw in the hen-house where Karl had also hidden the airman's gear. This was rapidly moved to a store of illegal weapons at a school in Holbæk. Soon after a German patrol stopped on the road outside Karl's workshop and started shouting about an Englishman while pointing at a green line leading from the workshop to the spot where Jimmy had landed. When Karl had fetched Jimmy's gear in the thicket he had overlooked the fact that a small pouch containing green, luminescent powder had been torn apart and now this powder was staring everybody in the face as a stripe across his field and adjoining road. The blacksmith went out to the patrol and explained that the powder was a special fertilizer spilt from one of his farm implements. Happy with this luminous explanation the pair of *Feldwebel* departed.

Now Esther picked up Jimmy and escorted him to the railway station at Vipperød. As the train from Holbæk destined for Roskilde stopped at the platform, Esther signalled to a passenger who was opening a window and escorted Jimmy into his compartment. This passenger was P.K. Jensen. Like Christian he had a hunch that he was wanted by the *Gestapo*. In the compartment the other passengers who embarked on the train at Vipperød were chatting, wondering what had become of the forlorn British flyers. P.K. pretended to join this conversation candidly while Jimmy, now dressed in civilian clothes, sat in a corner, reading his newspaper. At Roskilde they went to see Aage Nørfelt (age 40), the principal of a secondary school. Just like P.K. he was the local head of *Ringen* and also head of the Roskilde committee of *Danmarks Frihedsråd*. He was the second to last link in the network before Copenhagen for all escape lines of which local clergymen were the tentacles whom all RAF-airmen had been instructed to approach. The code word giving access to this network was RAF-aelsen (a Danish surname). The last link was a person without a name having his residence at Nørrevoldgade in Copenhagen. An anonymous Englishman has described the networks as follows:

Summary report on the organising of escape lines from Denmark.
In the summer of 1944 the organisation *Ringen* was charged with organising escape lines from Denmark for allied pilots.

In cooperation with the organisation of clergymen, PUF, (the unofficial union of clergymen) a network was laid covering Denmark as a whole. Chief organisers were for *Ringen* Professor Erik Husfelt, Copenhagen, Arthur Hansen, provinces, and Professor Ege, shipping. For PUF Pastor Th. Glahn and pastor N.J. Rald. Courier informed the clergymen as were the members of *Ringen* and a password was chosen. The clergymen passed on the information to as many clergymen inside their district as they were sure of, thus in all covering about 95% of the Danish clergy. Each of these clergymen was charged with the safe delivery of allied pilots to the nearest member of *Ringen* who in his turn took upon him to bring the pilots another step further ending with Copenhagen where the pilots were billeted awaiting the departure of boats bound for Sweden. In each case identity cards and civilian clothes were supplied either by members of *Ringen* or the PUF.

In some cases the pilots were not brought to Copenhagen owing to the control of the *Gestapo* of the ferry steamers, but were sent off to Sweden by other routes (Frederikshavn, Grenå, Vejle).

A number of pilots were sent off by other organisations of which we have no record. Fortunately there were not enough pilots to go round with the result that quite a number of the members both of *Ringen* and PUF never had a chance of giving the assistance they were ready to give.

Source: The Museum of Danish Resistance, Archives, F-10.

However, Aage was at school when P.K. rang the bell, and Ulla, his wife, for security reasons had no clue of the existence of RAF-aelsen. So, she was taken aback when she opened the door and saw Jimmy. She called her husband on the phone and was asked to hide the Englishman well. Rigmor, the maid, took Jimmy to a guest room in the far end of the house. She cooked eggs and bacon for the wretched airman and retold to him what she had just heard from the censored news about the miserable fate of the crew. Jimmy was now put up for the night. He slept like a log and passed into the land of dreams although the central heating system made the room uncomfortably warm for an Englishman unused to it.

One may wonder why Rev. Johannesen let his wife go by bike to Holbæk and walk Jimmy to the railway station rather than taking the turn himself. After all, Paul was the contact person for the network, while Esther was the mother of three children aged 7, 4, and 2. The answer rests on a consideration of security. Every Thursday morning Paul received his class of confirmands for preparation at the vicarage. In a situation of excitement like this any deviation from his daily routine

Rev. Paul With Johannesen and Esther, Sønder Asmindrup, their four children and housemaid (right), 1955.
Source: private archive.

56

like cancelling his class might attract the suspicion of the neighbourhood, particularly, since it had been aroused already by his ill-concealed allusions to national vacillation in his sermons. Apparently, the precautionary measures taken by Paul and Esther were not at all exaggerated.

Less than two weeks before the crash Paul and Esther had been made aware of an ominous episode. On 2nd February the dead body of a young woman wrapped in a dressing gown had been found in a lake, Maglesø, in the southern part of their parish. An old fisherman, living on the edge of the lake, had found the corpse, which surfaced as he broke a hole in the ice to spear eels. The death certificate Paul had received from the district medical officer for entry into the parish register was replete with question marks. The only data available were place and date of finding as well as approximate age: c. 30 years. A few days later a courier from the Resistance, a detective constable who had gone underground after the German imprisonments of the police corps turned up at the vicarage. He told Paul that the Resistance had kept all personal information relating to this woman as well as the intentions behind her hiring a room at Sindahls Pension, a boarding house at nearby Tølløse. The woman had been liquidated according to a 'death sentence' of 6th January '45 by secret order of *Danmarks Frihedsråd*, he said. She appeared to be a beautiful young, red-haired woman, only 21 years old. She frequently travelled by train to associate herself with German officers at Tølløse Baptist High School, requisitioned by the occupying forces. Her intentions had been disclosed as selling lists of names of individuals suspected of combating the Germans. Esther and Paul were shocked to learn that they were both on her list. A Resistance group from Copenhagen had entered the boarding house and had the girl called for under the pretence that somebody wanted to talk to her on the phone, when they had strangled her and taken her by motorcycle to Maglesø where she was dumped.

✵ ✵ ✵ ✵ ✵

Jim, the rear gunner, had been carried away in his parachute and landed some four miles away from his mates. As already mentioned he had left the aircraft first, from a high altitude and from a more easterly position.

Jim & Olive Petre, son James, and daughter Patricia, December '42. Only Jim survives.
Source: private archive.

His descent took about nine minutes, he was afterwards told. Nine minutes suspended in one clip and surrounded by dense clouds was ample time to worry whether he would fall into the sea to survive for only a few more minutes or be lucky enough to come down on land. The territory below him – if territory it be – would be completely blacked out, so when he broke through layers of clouds he saw three pinpricks of light which took the pattern of a triangle. Jim imagined they radiated from lighthouses. For a few seconds he thought, 'this is it. I'm going to land in the sea'. He then remembered being instructed to relax completely before hitting the ground and doing so he landed in a small meadow – without injury.

Quickly, he gathered his parachute together and lay on it for thirty minutes or so watching the activity of the Germans searching for the crew. Remembering his training he planned his next move, which was to dispose of his parachute. He walked to the edge of the meadow and crossed a small stream (Elverdamsåen) into a wooded area approximately twenty yards or so, and buried his parachute with the aid of a small single bladed knife. This took him about an hour and he made a good job of it, indeed, because the chute remained hidden in the bank until it was retrieved several years later.

Everything had gone according to plan so far, so it was only right that he made his first mistake. A new type of flying boot – different from the ones lost by Roy on his descent – had been issued to Jim. They were shoes with an upper suede sheepskin lining. The stitching had to be cut with a knife leaving the airman with a pair of shoes. He would then have to dispose of the uppers. He now decided on his plan of action. With the aid of a compass contained in his 'Pandora' he intended to get away from the scene of the crash as quickly as possible with a view to travelling eastwards in an attempt to cross to Sweden. It was then he realised his mistake. By cutting off the uppers of his flying boots, the resulting 'shoes' turned out to be too big and kept slipping off his feet, which meant he had to retrace his steps continually to find them. This was not easy and, in addition, his feet were quite cold and wet.

'Skovager', Lars Peter Larsen's smallholding at Skovvejen 4, near Ryegaard. Source: private archive.

After walking for a few hours along edges of fields steering purposely clear of the roads Jim decided to make his first contact. He came upon a small clump of cottages and knocked on the two-piece door of the end house saying 'l'anglais' and 'RAF'. The smallholders refused to open the door and Jim guessed they were telling him to go away. So he did, as fast as he could for fear they would send for the Germans. There was snow in the bottom of the dykes and he swallowed handfuls to quench his thirst. Walking throughout the night he realised he must make contact with someone before dawn broke as by now he was exhausted and very hungry. Pondering his next move he suddenly saw a chink of light at a farmhouse about 300 yards away and thought 'This is it!'

Approaching the light he saw through a window the farmer busy milking. He then followed around to the living quarters of the farm where he saw the farmer's wife and knocked nervously on the two-piece

Jim in his new Danish clothes, photographed at 'Skovager' by Lars Peter 15th February '45. Source: private archive.

door. The woman opening the upper half gave a sharp cry, then closed the door again to dash to the cattle shed and notify her husband. Should Jim take his chance and wait or should he make away like he had already done once? To his credit the farmer pulled Jim into his living room and offered him an opportunity to explain himself. He became aware then that his face was caked in dry blood. It must have been when his parachute caught his face during the escape through the turret. This was obviously the reason why the farmer's wife cried out when she first saw him.

The farmer, Lars Peter Larsen (age 54), even speaking no English, proved most helpful. Jim took out his silk maps explaining that he was an RAF pilot and pointing at the kitchen range to make the couple understand that his aircraft had been shot down in flames. Their position on the map was identified. It was No. 4, Skovvejen; the name of the smallholding was 'Skovager' indicating its vicinity to a forest. It was one of several plots that had been parcelled out from the estate of Ryegaard in 1920, when Lars Peter had bought it. Jim told the Larsens that he was aiming to rest until six o'clock p.m. when he would head for Copenhagen and try to find a boat to take him to Sweden. Lars Peter and Agnes, his wife, gave a wry smile probably thinking that the Englishman was mad. Jim was promptly given a large jug of milk, which never left his lips until it had gone. This was followed by a mountainous breakfast of bacon, three eggs, etc. His hunger completely satisfied he pointed to the clock and indicated by signs that he would sleep until six o'clock and then leave the farm. By this time Lars Peter had given Jim a suit, a pair of lace-up boots, a Macintosh, and a cap. Jim's boots were put in a bag and buried in the dunghill, but after the liberation Lars Peter dug them up again and wore them for many years when working outdoors or driving his car.

He was then taken up into the hayloft, covered over and left to sleep until early evening. Soon before that, however, heavy steps leading to the hayloft and Lars Peter shouting 'Help has come, help has come' interrupted his slumber! But what kind of help? Germans? Danish authorities? No need to worry, however. Enter Count F.C.R. Scheel, Ryegaard, a most elegant and imposing person, who assured Jim in fluent English

Count F.C.R. Scheel, Ryegaard. Source: private archive.

that his worries were now over and that he would be returned to England. Count Scheel was a member of the local Resistance and he had made his estate a store for weapons brought from the Barracks of Roskilde, which the Germans had occupied since 29th August '43. These weapons were concealed for the eventual use by freedom fighters. The Count had now taught Lars Peter his first few words of English: 'Help has come!'

From now on events moved quite quickly. At about noon Carl Petersen, a taxi driver, and another person arrived and took Jim to Roskilde. Carl Petersen's taxi was often used by Count Scheel and other Resistance members because he had clandestine access to petrol, so his car was only equipped with a gas producer for the sake of appearances. It had to be kept burning, of course, but the car was driven by normal fuel. As they entered the town of Roskilde they had to follow Fælledvej, a road passing through the training ground of the Barracks of Roskilde seized by German troops. They passed it just as a column of German military vehicles set out in the opposite direction to search for the allied airmen. At Roskilde they met Mogens Scheel, Count Scheel's brother, at 63, Frederiksborgvej; Mogens Scheel (age 42) was a timber merchant and Jim remembers him as an elegant and charming with a goatee. The fugitive was put up for one night at Mogens's weekend cottage close to the Bay of Roskilde. Jim's plan of evasion to Sweden had now been taken over by friendly hands, which made the RAF-lad feel rather more relieved.

DANISH COLLABORATION & THE GERMAN LUFTWAFFE

At the outbreak of the Second World War the Danish government reaffirmed its neutral status, which had carried the country through the First World War so successfully. The occupation of Denmark on 9th April 1940 was not directed against an enemy, however insignificant, nor was it primarily motivated by a German interest in the country per se. The occupation was considered a necessary step to secure a supply line towards Norway. Norway was important for her coastline facing the Atlantic and for her ice-free harbours from which Swedish iron ore was shipped to the German war industries. In other words: Denmark was a stepping stone, a territory necessary and ideal for airfields for stopovers without which the German conquest of Norway would have been technically impossible. The number one target of 9th April '40 was Aalborg airfield, which was taken by surprise by German parachutists early in the morning. It was not even guarded by Danish military, and the Government had called off all military resistance against the invading forces, anyway.

Later that day a huge fleet of German bombers accompanied by transport aircraft landed in Aalborg only to refuel and to act as an air bridge on which additional ground forces and fuel supplies could be flown to Stavanger, Oslo and other Norwegian airfields further north. This was the largest air bridge yet seen in history. Hundreds of tons of fuel in twenty litre cans and more than five hundred aircraft transported two hundred litre barrels. Following the German seizure of Western Scandinavia, Aalborg was turned into a huge airbase, and the expansion of existing airfields and construction of entirely new airbases was initiated with the purpose of a complete German mastery of the air theatre of Denmark and Norway. The German strategy was to launch strikes against allied convoys, submarines and mine sowing operations as well as against Britain herself.

The neutrality of Denmark, which the Germans had been so considerate to protect, and her insignificance in the theatre of war, however, did by no means nullify her part in the all-encompassing life-and-death struggle between Hitler's Germany and Great Britain. Already in April the German occupying forces decided to construct from scratch a large airfield on the moor at Grove in Jutland. Two groups of contractors (Christiani & Nielsen and Monberg & Thorsen) refused to cooperate in Denmark with Organisation Todt (OT), a Para-military section of the German Government responsible for the construction of military works and for the reparation of damaged infrastructure in Germany and occupied territories. The reason for this refusal is unknown, but it was hardly ideological since both firms were already engaged in construction work in Hamburg. On inquiry to the coalition government, however, Wright, Thomsen & Kier were encouraged to take on the work. So were contractors generally. Prime Minister Th. Stauning and John Christmas Møller, leader of the Conservatives, argued that it was preferable if a Danish company undertook the job rather than a German one employing Danish workers or, still worse, importing German labour in a situation of Danish mass unemployment. Wright, Thomsen & Kier, however, were by no means forced to comply, and other Danish companies, e.g. Bang & Olufsen, refused to work for the Germans throughout the occupation – and paid the price for it, too, when their factory in Struer was razed to the ground.

Soon a Danish work force of more than ten thousand men, recruited from all over the country was changing the desolate moor into a busy construction site. The wages were very attractive. Skilled workers were paid twice the normal wages, and since concrete bunkers and landing strips had to be cast in one go, overtime labour was a must for which the workmen received double pay. The high wages enabled them to pay the exorbitant prices for accommodation, and after the depression of the thirties the construction business was a welcome boost to the local economy. Neither the OT nor Wright, Thomsen & Kier had any reason to complain of high wages, since the National Bank of Denmark paid all bills.

Fliegerhorst Grove comprised twenty-four hangars, sixty-one split-ter-boxes, workshops, roads, barracks, anti-aircraft batteries, and a railway linking it with Aalborg, which had been enlarged on a similar scale. It should be borne in mind that this was not a result of forced labour. In other countries the OT would take advantage of POWs, Polish and Russian, in particular – and concentration camp prisoners. Slave labour was not necessary in Denmark where government, unions, entrepreneurs and workers all volunteered. It has subsequently been claimed by many Danes working for the Germans and by some historians, too, that these jobs whether in Denmark or in Germany must be considered forced labour. But there was no physical force involved. Economic incitement was sufficient.

Already from mid-'40 standards of living started to improve considerably around Flieghorst Grove and the Western Wall. Employment in-

The 'Gyges' Bunker at Gedhus (near Grove) under construction '43. Illegal photo, smuggled out in a thermos. Source: Flyvestation Karups Historiske Forening (B12-1319-43).

creased and thousands of male and female workers swarmed at the construction site and in the workshops and kitchens of the airfield. Locals possessing means of transport or lodgings to hire out profited and fraternization was common. The workmen had to sign a document – OT's *Verpflichtungserklärung* – thereby submitting themselves to German law, i.e. declaring that they did not belong to the Jewish race, committing themselves to perform their duties loyally towards the Wehrmacht and to report immediately to their employers any sign of espionage or sabotage against German facilities.

There is no in-depth investigation of the history of the Danish working class during the war. Tens of thousands of workers volunteered to work for the Germans in Germany or at German fortifications in Denmark. The illegal press warned Danish workers against voluntary recruitment to work in Germany at German employment offices set up in Denmark. The warnings were accompanied by deterrent examples that wages and work conditions in Germany did not live up to the promises given by the employment offices. In case hired workers complained to their German employers they put themselves at risk of being sent to rehabilitation- or concentration camps, where, as is well-known, they were treated as slaves. The warning hardly made a significant impact. It was probably far more efficient to threaten the unemployed that they would very likely lose their dole – restricted to last no longer than one year – if they refused to take on an assigned job in Denmark (but not in Germany). In case the right to receive unemployment relief had been forfeited social benefits were the last resort; but in the event of continuous refusal to take on an assigned job in Denmark benefits were liable to cuts and, furthermore, the beneficiary would lose the right to vote.

In fact a large proportion of the Danish population acquiesced in the occupation of their country by regarding the German troops as providers of gains rather than as usurpers of freedom. As a journalist communicated to John Christmas-Møller, Minister of Commerce, 'When taking a look at the works of construction I talked to one of the workers. He was enthusiastic about the Germans; before their arrival he had had to make do with social relief, whereas now he had regular employment. True, he had to work hard but that did not matter to him as long as he

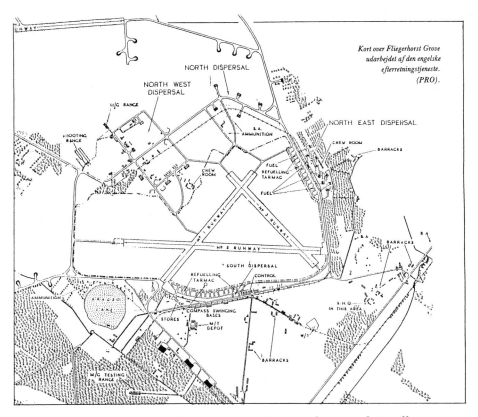

Fliegerhorst Grove in aerial perspective, drawing by British Intelligence. Source: Public Record Office, Kew, London, copied from Carsten Petersen, Luftkrig over Danmark, Jagerkontrol 1943-1945, Karup 1940-1945, Bollerup Boghandels Forlag, Ringkøbing 1988, p.91.

was well paid. The Danish model had been unable to provide him with a job, whereas the German system was very successful in this respect. According to him, this was the general attitude of members of Social Democratic unions in the 'red' town of Esbjerg.' In August '43 – after the turn in the fortunes of war – the Resistance movement could threaten with sabotage the steadily growing number of Danish employees to make them stop working for the Germans, without any repercussions being taken against the workmen who quitted. By mid-'43, however, full employment prevailed.

In August '40 the airbase (today's NATO Command, H.Q. Baltap, Karup) was ready to receive squadrons of bombers and fighters. It was immediately used as a point of departure for raids on British airfields, such as Driffield, on industrial plants and on the home fleet base of Scapa Flow in the Orkney Islands. At that time the *Luftwaffe* believed that British fighters were busily engaged in Southern England defending London and that consequently it would be easy for the German eagle to destroy the lion's den. On 15th August fifty Junkers left Grove like a string of pearls – according to lieutenant Rupps Kraz in the *Luftwaffe* Yearbook '41. Before their sortie they had been briefed with photos of Driffield airbase, now destined to be turned into a heap of scrap. The Junkers penetrated the showers of British flaks, dropped their bombs, and made ten Whitley-planes whirl through the air like tin clippings. What Rupps Kraz is tacit about are German losses of the same number of Junkers shot down or severely damaged by Hurricanes, which were indeed on the alert. On this day alone raids on British factories, cities, and airbases, Driffield being merely one of them, caused the loss of forty-three RAF aircraft, but the *Luftwaffe* lost ninety aircraft of their own. Rupps Kraz does mention, however, his own relaxation and complacency during his safe return to Denmark.

Later on the *Luftwaffe* continued their attacks on northern and eastern England, such as Scarborough, Middlesborough, and Sunderland as well as targets in Scotland, including Scapa Flow. Convoys and merchant vessels were frequently attacked from Aalborg and Grove airbases. *Fliegerhorst Grove* used almost two hundred aircraft for training pilots, navigators, and gunners and the Messerschmidt fighters for operational purposes as well. From July '42 new squadrons of Junker night fighters were stationed there. After the turn in the theatre of war in Europe, Danish air territory like that of the Low Countries constituted an advanced guard of German air defence.

In May '43, however, a Junkers fighter took off from Grove airfield with most unexpected repercussions. The crew of three reported to the radar station at Klitmøller on the west coast of Jutland that their engine

Junkers fighter Ju88R-1, D5-EV, equipped with Lichtenstein radar and radio, and deserting to England. Source: The Royal Air Force Museum, Hendon.

was on fire over the North Sea and that they would attempt an emergency landing. 'Please drop a rubber boat!' Reconnaissance proved as futile as rescue. The Junker, a brand new type equipped with *Lichtenstein*, the most updated version of German radar systems, was missing and the sad loss of an experienced crew was reported to their forlorn families. The Mayday signal, however, was a whopper. For personal reasons two of the three German flight officers were clandestine anti-nazis who had never hit a single RAF-aircraft although they had had plenty of opportunities during the Battle of Britain. A pistol silenced the protests of the third crewmember, who was not initiated into the plan. Approaching Peterhead, the easternmost point of Scotland, the Junkers was intercepted by two Spitfires. The deserters lowered their undercarriage – an internationally approved indication of surrender of aircraft – and landed safely close to Aberdeen.

This Junkers aircraft was literally a gift from heaven to RAF intelligence. During a recent raid on German radar stations Bomber Command had learned the exact wavelength of the enemy's radar screens and transmitters. It was now discovered that *Lichtenstein* used exactly the same one. This knowledge made the German air defence most vulnerable to RAF attacks. Two retaliatory measures offered themselves. Firstly, noise jamming would disturb not only German ground stations using *Würzburg* radar, but also the *Lichtenstein* system on board German night fighters and the communication between the two. Secondly, the dispersal of *window*, i.e. small tin-foil strips cut into the same size as the wavelengths used by the radar equipment would make RAF-aircraft invisible to hostile fighters. The deserters had provided British intelligence with a tool to nullify German air defence and to penetrate with much less risk into the heartland of the Third Reich.

On top of this, the RAF was informed by their defector friends of the organisation and technology of *Fliegerhorst Grove* and of the offensive and defensive strategies of *Luftwaffe*. The two talkative officers were now transferred to the BBC to broadcast propaganda for the allied cause and to demoralize the enemy. Bomber Command took major advantage by drawing up operation *Gomorrah*, a grand-scale air bombardment of Hamburg. Let us be reminded of Genesis 19, 24-28, 'Then the Lord rained upon... Gomorrah... fire from the Lord out of heaven; and he overthrew those cities... and all the inhabitants of the cities... And Abraham... looked toward... Gomorrah... and beheld, and lo, the smoke of the country went up as the smoke of a furnace.' During the last week of July '43 when the duration of the dark of the night was still short and the temperature of the day still high, British armadas of aircraft numbering nearly eight hundred each night dropped thousands of tons of phosphorous bombs and high-explosive bombs over Hamburg. The German radar screens had indicated that 11,000 bombers were passing Helgoland and heading towards the city. So, obviously, their warning systems were out of function. The *Luftwaffe*'s *Jägerkommando* was utterly confused to learn that the fifty-four flak stations and twenty-two searchlight stations protecting their best defended city were useless against the intruding bombers which had turned into invisible targets to the gunners of their night fighters. Whereas the RAF usually expected a loss of eight per cent of their air force, these attacks on Hamburg only cost two per cent, mainly aircraft that for different reasons had failed to follow the stream. The actual droppings lasted less than an hour but the devastation was horrific. And this was only the prelude to the carpet-bombing of more major cities with the purpose of transforming the Third Reich to the last Reich. We shall return to the casualties and other effects of *Gomorrah* in due course when we shall face the bitterness against RAF-Tommie's that it fostered.

'Bomber-Harris' had reckoned that *Gomorrah* would convince Hitler that German cities were defenceless against the RAF. But he had made a miscalculation. In response to the shock caused by the Hamburg disaster the Germans decided in August '43 to build a new command

The 'Gyges' Bunker, '48.
Source: Flyvestation Karups Historiske Forening (B6-776-FTh-48).

bunker. This was *Zentralgefechtsstand* 'Gyges' (named after a tyrant ruler of ancient Greece) situated in the vicinity of *Fliegerhorst* Grove and it became the operation centre alerting Husemann and Schierholz. It was completed by January '44 and was by far the biggest bunker in Denmark. Together with 'Socrates' near Stade (Hamburg) and 'Diogenes' (named after another Greek founding the Cynic sect) near Arnhem in the

The 'Gyges' Bunker. Control centre manpowered by air traffic controllers, wireless operators, searchlight-, radar-, and flak-operators.
Source: Flyvestation Karups Historiske Forening (B6-730-Bk-1137-45).

Netherlands this bunker constituted the main control centre for German air operations in Northern Europe. It went well underground and eighteen metres above ground level. It measured fifty-four by sixty-eight metres and was constructed in heavily reinforced concrete so as to be virtually indestructible. Yet, camouflage netting covered the entire building.

The sector operations centre employed personnel of about three thousand people. Apart from a meteorological section it coordinated all radar surveillance to the centre and communication from the centre to other airfields. The heart of the bunker was a huge operation centre equipped with a glass screen map of Denmark and her seas, twelve metres by fifteen, where all observations of intruding aircraft were plotted in on their correct positions. From here night fighter operations were commanded. The staff (partly women) plotted information with light beams to monitor signals and reports from radar stations. On the other side of the glass screen were officers issuing orders to fighters on alert at Grove or at other airfields or in the air. After the liberation, British officers inspecting the seized command bunker had to obtain directions for the use of this abstruse system from the former German staff. The general impression after a simulated British attack, the *Post Mortem* rehearsal in '45, was that the advantage of this system was out of proportion to the number of staff employed.

It would have been interesting to know how Major Werner Husemann and his navigator, Hans-Georg Schierholz, thrived at Karup during the occupation. Schierholz is no longer alive, but Husemann is. Unfortunately he refuses to communicate with his victims as well as with historians approaching him with letters totally devoid of bad feelings. So, unfortunately, there is no way of imparting the event from his point of view – fascinating, as it would no doubt be. It is known, though, that he became engaged to a Danish girl living at Ålborg, from whence she was flown out of Denmark by the last German aircraft to leave Denmark on the day of liberation, 5th May '45, to settle down with him as his wife amidst the ruins and to spend the rest of her life in Germany. Husemann has outlived her.

CAPTURE OR EVASION?

FRIDAY 16TH – DAY THREE

TWO PATIENTS

In their hospital beds Stan and Andy were waiting to be picked up by P.K. Of course it was simple for the Germans or their Danish minions to figure out that the two airmen might be assisted in escaping from the hospital. Holbæk police station, a few hundred yards away, was housing the Gestapo, who were collaborating closely with Ole Heike and Ib Birkedal Hansen. Heike was the leader of the local Danish Nazi-party, and one of the informers engaged by Ib Birkedal Hansen, the abominable terrorist, with his own office at Dagmarhus, and Nina Danielsen, his fiancée. There were other informers, too. For instance there was Holbæk Frøkompagni, a seed company, known locally as a Nazi-nest, and among those certain Holbæk females who made a living by cleaning, sewing and cooking for the Germans at the Barracks of Holbæk and at the Mine Testing Station, when not providing them with more frivolous services. Informing was commonplace, informers were generously paid for their regular reports to Gestapo Headquarters (two hundred Danish kroner a fortnight, equal to a workman's pay), and the Germans' insight into local Resistance activities was profound. Two informers were liquidated by the freedom fighters and forced escort rendered others harmless to Sweden. But once the unravelling of Resistance groups was initiated, i.e. groups receiving weapons or explosives dropped by Special Operations Executive or making sabotage on manufactories or railways, the complete rolling up of the entire organisation was almost unavoidable. The Germans had recently been successful in tracing stores of weapons; they had rolled up Resistance groups, arrested and tortured them in great numbers, and blown up their private homes.

Now, on the second day of their involuntary sojourn at Holbæk, Stan and Andy could just lie down and hope for P.K. to turn up. It required some courage and skill from doctors and nurses to hide the British patients, and some Danish hospitals made successful efforts at this. Holbæk was not among them. We shall probably never get to know exactly what happened at the hospital since the evidence is lost. The hospital administration has communicated its inability to retrieve the files, which might have provided the answer, if they ever existed. We do know, however, the sad outcome of this hospitalisation.

Friday afternoon or evening German troopers carrying rifles and wearing boots marched into the hospital ward to ascertain that the Tommie's were present, whereupon they left the room, apparently to be on the watch at a suitable place to seize P.K. Jensen. Unwittingly, he was trapped and arrested at the very moment he showed up at the hospital after having escorted Jimmy to Roskilde. Straight away Stan and Andy, too, were seized by the Gestapo and handed over to the *Seekriegsmarine* as POWs. In other words, P.K. did what he could and paid the price. He was interrogated and imprisoned at the Town Hall of Holbæk, but remained silent as to where and whom he came from. He was transferred to Police Head Quarters in Copenhagen where he caught glimpses of some of his comrades from the Resistance. He did not get a chance to talk to them.

Stan and Andy were soon transferred to a room in a cellar, probably at The Mine Testing Station on the coast a few miles from Holbæk. A young German Naval Rating gave them two slices of black bread each, of which they could eat nothing, and a bottle of milk which they enjoyed. During the night their captors brought their girlfriends in to taunt the prisoners, but Stan being a former Liverpool dock worker and knowing a thing or two gave them some comments that they probably did not understand and eventually they departed. Still weak from their injuries there was little they could do to resist captivity save stick together, which they did.

Stan & Hilda Chaderton, marriage '45.
Source: private archive

THREE EVADERS

Early Friday morning Roy and Hanse were ready to leave on foot for Tølløse and to travel by train together to Carl Syrach-Larsen at Charlottenlund. Although Tølløse railway station was five miles away, it was preferred to Vipperød next to the farmhouses since Germans were still combing these. Roy looked almost Danish in his new suit. Upon leaving Havremarken they observed two, armed *Feldwebel* approaching the house up the driveway. They rushed back inside and Roy was pushed through the shutter to the loft and hidden in a large cupboard. Hanse sent Rigborg out to ask the Germans what they wanted. '*Eier, Eier, haben Sie Eier?*' ('Eggs, eggs, do you have any eggs?'). Quickly, Rigborg fetched some new laid eggs and handed them out to the soldiers who put down their guns, swallowed the raw eggs, and walked away happier than they arrived. Breathing a sigh of relief Roy reappeared and off he was accompanied by his host along fences and across fields towards Tølløse.

When the train arrived they entered an empty compartment and sat down in opposite corners reading newspapers. For obvious reasons they couldn't talk. Roy was very nervous and had been told to try to look less nervous. Then two SS-soldiers entered. Soon they were engaged in conversation not noticing that Roy was reading his Danish newspaper upside down. Syrach-Larsen had warned Hanse not to disembark at the Central Station of Copenhagen, which was meticulously guarded by Germans, so they changed to the S-train at Valby for Charlottenlund where they arrived without difficulty. Hanse went back to Havremarken relieved that his dear windfall (this was a term often used by freedom fighters about allied flyers) had come a small step further on his home run.

Carl Syrach-Larsen, head of the arboretum, had a study in a half-timbered house in the garden. This was a quiet place where Carl had been working on his dissertation, and here Roy was put up for the night. As Carl left him he crashed a windowpane from the outside to make Roy's presence appear like that of an intruder who had forced his way into the shed. Carl felt that there was no need to jeopardize his family. His forest botanical institute was close to the Sound and served as a 'well-box' to a range of refugees such as Jews, freedom fighters, and allied airmen waiting for a passage to Sweden, and he was cooperating with a range of key figures. Among them was Professor Richard Ege, who was providing falsified identity papers, as well as Vice-Admiral Aage H. Vedel, who in August '43 had given orders to sink the Danish Navy, under the very eyes of the German occupying forces, and who was now working illegally for 'Elverhøj', the Navy's intelligence agency, as well as organising escape routes to Sweden. Vedel was the godfather of Lise, Carl and Nina's daughter, and a frequent guest of the family. Lise remembers Vedel as being tight as a clam. Under the circumstances, Roy spent a quiet night in relative safety.

*****

What happened to Jimmy, now in Roskilde, when he woke up Friday morning, while P.K. was supposed to have returned to Holbæk the previous day? Aage Nørfelt and Christian Kirkegaard, a good friend of his, accompanied Sgt. Mills alias Mr. Hansen on a train from Roskilde to the Central Station of Copenhagen. They were sharing the same compartment, but couldn't be sitting next to one another. Jimmy had been told that in case of a German raid on the train he would be left on his own, his helpers being helpless. Jimmy sat reading the news or rather glaring at a paper when the ticket inspector routinely asked him if he intended to extend his journey from the central station by the S-train. Jimmy looked puzzled. The ticket inspector repeated his question and the RAF pilot in disguise continued to look puzzled. Then the inspector punched the ticket as if he had smelled a rat. The route from the Central Station to Nørrevoldgade passed by the Gestapo headquarters in Shellhuset and the German headquarters, Dagmarhus, housing the offices of Dr. Werner Best, *SS-Obergruppenführer* and Hitler's *Reich Plenipotentiary* of Denmark. What a thrill of pleasure – and horror – for all three men to walk past the German sentries.

As they reached Nørrevoldgade Jimmy was left on the street while Aage went up to find out whom the last link of the chain was. Who would open the door of this cover address? Would the Resistance embrace him or would the Gestapo arrest him? A lady answered the bell and Aage introduced himself as 'Ove RAF-aelsen' from Roskilde. 'Are you alone?' 'Well, I have an escort on the street.' 'Give him the green light!' Jimmy was brought into the flat and welcomed by Richard Ege and his wife. Richard was a professor of medicine working for the Rockefeller Institute in Copenhagen. He and his wife had been a driving force behind the rescue of the Danish Jews in October '43, organizing finance, transportation, falsification of documents, etc. By February '45 they had long been living underground. Jimmy and Aage could breathe again. The RAF-aelsen-network appeared to work safely – at least so far.

When Aage returned to Roskilde, however, he was warned by a telephone call from Rev. Krarup-Hansen, Butterup, one of the leading clergymen of the network, that the Gestapo at Holbæk had arrested a fellow plotter of his, 'Ove Rafelsen' from Holbæk. In other words, an important link in the network, P.K., was under arrest. As a consequence, would he be able to keep silent about the RAF-aelsen line? If not Jimmy was in imminent danger. Right now he was left in caring hands, but for how long? If tortured by the Gestapo could P.K. succeed in keeping their attention fixed on the two patients and leave them in ignorance about RAF-aelsen and Jimmy?

* * * * *

This morning Jim was escorted to the Hafnia Hotel, No. 23, Vester Voldgade, in the city of Copenhagen by Carl Petersen, the taxi driver who had delivered him from 'Skovager' to Mogens Scheel's house at Roskilde the previous day. In Copenhagen two more members of the underground joined. After coffee and schnapps Jim was asked if he would like to take a look around the city. Little did he know that he was offered a sightseeing tour of Copenhagen. After the initial shock he agreed, thinking that if the Danes dared take the risk so did he. Walking through the streets of Copenhagen they came upon a photographer, and Georg Suhr asked Jim if he would like a photograph taken to which he readily agreed. They then had a beer in a local bar awaiting the film being developed. The first go was a failure so they posed again, this time successfully. Playing what was almost a prank on the Germans was no doubt a foolhardy thing to do. The point, of course, was not the sightseeing or the prank per se. What really mattered was the enjoyment of being together. The Resistance people wanted to demonstrate to the RAF flyer what it meant to be victimized by the Nazis by showing them Shellhuset, Dagmarhus, sabotaged factories, etc., what Resistance groups were aiming at and how their comrades were put to suffer for it. Doing that, established ties between allies and strengthened their morale and awareness of their mutual objectives.

After their walkabout in the city they returned to the Hafnia Hotel where a lunch attended by several underground members had been arranged in Jim's honour. The dining room was partitioned, the allied party in one half and numerous German military in the other half. It lasted until late in the afternoon and the noise from both sides of the dining room was quite boisterous. It was dark when the party broke up. A stu-

Group picture, Copenhagen, 17.2.45. Jim is No. 2 left. No.1 left is Ove Mandrup-Poulsen, an architect, who was leader of section II of Copenhagen region. After the war he was appointed lieutenant-colonel in the engineers. No.1 right is Georg Suhr, a policeman gone under ground. No. 2 right is an unknown taxi-driver. Source: private archive.

dent of chemistry then took Jim to his college to be put up for the night. Sadly, this anonymous freedom fighter later committed suicide. He had been ordered to kill a man accused of being an informer. Later on, however, he was worried whether the evidence was sufficient to prove that he had not, in fact, killed an innocent man by mistake.

POWs & ESCAPEES

SATURDAY 17TH
DAY FOUR & LATER

TWO PRISONERS OF WAR

After having spent the night in the cellar of the Barracks of Holbæk, Stan and Andy woke up facing the fact that they were German POWs and that from now on their lives were subjected to German command. On Sunday a coach powered by a wood burner took them to Værløse airfield, about ten miles northwest of Copenhagen. At Værløse Stan was admitted into the hospital where he was given treatment for his injuries. On the second day there Stan's face and fingers began to swell up and the doctor said he was allergic to the tetanus injection he had been given at Holbæk. He was given a calcium drip into his arm, which cleared it up. As POWs they were entitled to medical care according to the Geneva Convention, which Germany had signed and which Nazi-Germany fulfilled to the extent their resources allowed. As POWs they retained their RAF uniforms and were under no obligation to cooperate with their captors other than to state their name, rank, and number.

The two prisoners were well treated at Værløse. The German doctor aired his view that Germans and Britons ought to have fought on the same side rather than destroying one another. Such talk, however, scarcely changed the fact of their incarceration. From their infirmery ward Stan and Andy were watching German aircraft of transportation moving to and from the runway. Stan ventilated a suggestion of sneaking on board one of them to escape. He felt convinced that he could start and operate it.

But after about a week's recovery at Værløse Stan and Andy were transported under the escort of two armed guards to a boat sailing them to Rostock. They were put up in the bottom of the ship, where their situation mean instant death if the vessel ran into a mine in which case it would have been sown there by the RAF. From Rostock they were taken onwards by train to Hamburg. There was a delay at the Central Station, and hence there was plenty of time to look out of the window. They were facing a shocking spectacle, indeed. Miles of devastated streets and buildings caused by the *Gomorrah* raids met their eyes. Walking in RAF uniforms from one train to another they would very likely have been lynched by infuriated Hamburg citizens had they not been under the protection of their armed guards.

Their next destination was Frankfurt. During their journey allied aircraft attacked the train and all passengers were forced to get out and take cover in the fields. The steam locomotive was set ablaze, and only late at night a reserve came along to pull them on. German civilians on the run overcrowded the train. Some of them entered the compartment reserved for Stan, Andy and their guards. Had their guards not made efforts to protect them, they would probably have been thrown out through the door at full speed.

In Frankfurt another American daylight raid was on and they were ushered into a large shelter with German soldiers on each side. Sitting underground with the stern looks of hundreds of German civilians was a bit scary while the bombs were going off above them. When they resurfaced they witnessed an American airman, having been taken prisoner of war like themselves, being lynched by a furious mob of German citizens, their escorting guard giving up interference. He was hung in full uniform in a lamppost. In Nazi-Germany RAF-flyers were called 'Terrorflieger', and the Americans 'Air-gangsters'.

Finally, they arrived at *Dulag Luft*, ('Durchgangslager', transit camp) or the 'sweat box' as the Allied called it, which was the aircrew interrogation centre, where they were placed in solitary confinement for seven days. They slept on straw mattresses, if they slept at all. Central heating radiators were turned on and off systematically once an hour to break down their morale. They oscillated between states of shivering with cold and bathing in perspiration. There was one loo for several hundred prisoners. During this time a German officer who spoke perfect English and knew more about the 10 RAF Squadron than the two POWs themselves interrogated both. For instance, he had in front of him on his desk a RAF signal book complete with code translations and identical to the one Andy had lost above the 'Hjortholmsgaarden'. They were threatened with being handed over to the Gestapo as secret agents if they refused to cooperate, but the interrogation officer got nothing from them. All he got was their name, rang, and number in compliance with instructions and conventions.

Now, it must be remembered that whereas the German concentration camps run by the SS were confined to political prisoners; POW-camps were under the command of the German armed forces; and captured airmen were put into camps run by the *Luftwaffe*. Firstly, it is the general impression that American and Commonwealth POWs were treated far better than Soviet-Russians and Poles, mainly because the latter prisoners were taken in such large numbers that they greatly surpassed the capacity of the German *Wehrmacht*. Secondly, all airmen were treated as officers implying, according to the Geneva Convention that their captors were denied the option of employing them as forced labour, as opposed to the rank and file prisoners who were, more often than not, ordered to do hard labour in all sorts of jobs. The distinction between military and civil production was not easy to draw, particularly towards the end of the war. It is well known that most of the Polish POWs were exploited as forced labour and that more than two and a half million, or almost half of all Soviet POWs lost their lives in Germany either by being shot or by being starved to death. Since the Soviet Union had never signed the Geneva Convention, the Germans chose to define Soviet officers as political enemies and most of them were executed.

Under normal circumstances RAF aircrews belonged to the elite of POWs, although after the Allied invasion in Normandy, June '44, German authorities argued that the general scarcity of resources prevented them from fulfilling their obligations properly. In a situation when the entire German population suffered 'why should allied 'Kriegie' enjoy larger rations than the average German?' was the standard reply to complaints. 'Kriegie' was a term adopted by the POWs themselves. It was derived from the letters KG (*Kriegsgefangene*, POW), which all POWs had to wear on the jacket and trousers of their uniforms in large yellow letters. Compared to the conditions of army POWs from Eastern Europe, allied airmen were rather fortunate. But compared to normal circumstances living conditions in the *Stalag* were harsh. The *Dulag* near Frankfurt was a transit camp, and the *Stalag* was meant to be their permanent residence consisting of wooden barracks, watch towers, double barbed wire fences approaching which was strictly forbidden. The sentries, derogatively called 'goons' by Anglo-Saxon POWs, were instructed to fire without warning at any person who showed signs of intending to cross the warning wire some ten yards inside the ultimate fence. The watchtowers were equipped with searchlights and machine guns.

The POWs subsisted on Red Cross parcels from home and very few letters, which were censored by the camp authorities. During the winter and early springtime '45 about 40,000 American, British and Commonwealth airmen were imprisoned in seven camps. But as the Red army moved nearer from the east and the Allied Forces from the west, German camp commanding officers had instructions to evacuate their camps and move into pockets still controlled by the German *Wehrmacht*. This was now partly replaced by the *Volkssturm*, consisting of loyal party members, elderly men and young boys, Hitler's last desperate attempt to avoid final defeat. During this final evacuation everything was chaos. German 'goons' deserted, roads were crowded with refugees from the eastern parts of Germany, trains were packed, starving horses pulling carriages, women and children prostrate with fatigue and dysentery, while dead bodies and small fires were flanking the roads. The air was thick with rumours that Hitler would take advantage of Allied POWs by turning them into hostages to force concessions from the Allies under the peace negotiations to come.

After their uncomfortable experience at *Dulag Luft* Stan and Andy were taken to another camp nearby and given some clean clothes, another pair of boots, a shower and a meal. In return they suffered the indignity of having their heads shaved. From there they went by train to Nuremberg where they were marched to the northern outskirts and into *Stalag XIIID*. The camp was divided into five or six compounds, each compound consisting of five or six wooden huts. There were about a hundred POWs in each, but no beds, so, the 'Kriegie' were sleeping around the edge of the hut with one blanket each. This camp was neither designed to contain airmen nor officers. But this hardly mattered. Almost as soon as Stan and Andy arrived they were told by the 'goons' to prepare themselves for a long march. The Allies were advancing well into the German heartland, and the camp commander decided to put all aircrew on the road and march them towards Austria.

So, Stan and Andy collected together some of the contents of their Red Cross parcels and made emergency rations for what lay ahead. All POWs were formed up outside the camp. It took twenty-four hours for the whole column to form and move off. During the next sixteen days they suffered hunger, fatigue and cold. The wretched POWs slept in barns or under trees and hedges and they begged, bartered or stole food as they marched along. After a week the Red Cross obtained permission to supply food parcels directly from Switzerland and they did that regularly. Count Folke Bernadotte's white lorries carried supplies of Red Cross parcels, and the most weakened prisoners might be lucky enough to get a lift on the backboard. The evacuees, however, were attacked by American Thunderbolt aircraft despite putting down letters made of toilet paper spelling POW or RAF. German soldiers on the run played this trick as well, and the Americans fired at everything that moved. There were some casualties.

After more than a fortnight on the roads the German guards gave up moving the column, and consequently it was directed into *Stalag VIIA* at Moosburg to the northeast of Munich. This camp was already overcrowded containing about 45,000 POWs. Andy suffered from dysentery, his weight dropped to forty-five kilos and hence he depended very much on the help Stan was loyal enough to grant him. There were latrines in the camp. The distance from the spruce stems down to the clamp was about six yards. Andy was now so enfeebled by dysentery that one day he fainted in the stench tumbling into the pit. Stan and other co-prisoners got him picked up and flushed. At this stage, they had swopped roles.

They were liberated by Americans on 29th April, and the next day they heard about Hitler's suicide. The Americans were under command of general Patton, whose tough appearance and eccentric outfit: hyper-

Peter Frederick Andrews (Andy) as a POW. The photograph was taken at Dulag Luft, Frankfurt, ultimo February '45, just before his hair was shaved off. The No. 1811552 is the same as his RAF No.
Source: private archive.

polished boots, pearl-handled revolvers, and abundance of fruit salad on the chest of his uniform, excessively incarnated the myth of the blood-and-guts-general. He walked straight into the camp-commander's office, forced the archives open and put everything of Allied interest on a long self-service table. The liberated prisoners were then invited in to take their journals, photographs, and fingerprints and keep them as souvenirs.

However, Stan and Andy had to remain in the camp at Moosburg until they could be transported home. Trucks took them to an airfield outside Munich. The last act of war they witnessed was a German Stuka-fighter seeking to land, but being prevented by fire from the ground. The German pilot then let a white handkerchief flutter through the window as a sign of surrender, and the fire ceased. From Munich they were flown by an American Dakota to Rheims and from there by a Lancaster to Cosford in Oxfordshire where they were deloused, fed and given clean uniforms and new shoes. On 4th May Andy celebrated his 21st birthday and Stan, his 23rd some three weeks later. The war was over and they had both survived.

THREE ESCAPEES

Roy woke up in Carl's garden house on the 17th, still worried. Vice-Admiral Vedel, however, had paid a visit to the Syrach-Larsen family the evening before and had assigned the task of shipping Roy to Sweden to Poul L.S. Prom, a highly trusted naval officer, a member of 'Elverhøj', and a translator and interpreter of English. Poul picked up Roy at the arboretum and escorted him on the S-train to Copenhagen. At Hellerup station three men dressed in black and looking very sinister entered the compartment. 'Are they Gestapo?' Roy whispered. 'No, no, not at all'. Roy was told that these three gentlemen had probably just attended a funeral, and he calmed down.

Poul and Roy walked to Professor Ege's flat and false documents now transformed No. 2205669 Sgt. Roy Maddock-Lyon into Mr. Peter Jensen, 'assistant' by trade, living at No. 61, Nørre Farimagsgade, Copenhagen. A life-like photo was no problem since Roy had carried one with him in his escape-kit. Peter retained Roy's birthday as it was difficult to forget for the bearer of the identity card, should he be taken by surprise. Language was the problem and this could not be helped.

Roy was now better equipped to move around and the next two days he was sightseeing Copenhagen with his new host, Peter Bredsdorff, an architect of 31 and an Anglophile. Of course, Roy never set foot at No. 61, Nørre Farimagsgade, the address on his identity card, since this would be the first place his pursuers would look for him. Instead he was accommodated in Peter Bredsdorff's flat on the fifth floor, No. 89, Sortedams Dossering. Peter Bredsdorff was a member of the military group P6B belonging to the Resistance. Peter was studying British town and reconstruction planning in cooperation with Steen Eiler Rasmussen. On 28th February he published an illegal pamphlet entitled 'English Problems of Reconstruction'. Peter's wife, Ruth, had been a translator of English and a shorthand writer at the Danish Parliament, which had suspended itself on 29th August '43, and instead she had devoted herself to

Three freedom fighters from the architect group of 'Frit Danmark' outside Randersgade Skole, 5th May '45. Peter Bredsdorff in the middle, Mogens Boertmann to the left, and Esben Klint to the right.
Source: private archive.

the rescue of Danish Jews. This is how she got to know Professor Richard Ege well and started to help him sheltering allied escapees on the home run. So when Roy had had his identity papers issued at Richard's place he heard a voice on the phone calling somebody, 'I've got a box of chocolate for you'. Ruth was the receiver and the coded message meant that she was asked to come and pick up Roy. The following couple of days he was shown around to see the various buildings occupied by the Gestapo and other German military authorities, as well as the factories and other places devastated by sabotage groups.

On the 19th Roy was walked down to Havnegade, a street at the waterfront where passenger ships to and from Bornholm were loading

Roy's Danish identity cards. Roy Maddock-Lyon alias assistent Peter Jensen, Nørre Farimagsgade 61, København. Source: private archive.

and unloading. But before telling the story of Roy's escape route a few words must be said about the prevailing circumstances at the time of German occupation. The Sound was full of mines sown by the RAF in various sections of the sea each named after a flower, as you will remember. For this reason the normal sailing route to Bornholm, a Danish island in the Baltic, had been changed to pass through the Swedish Falsterbo Canal, not because it was shorter, but because it was safer. Secondly, fuel supplies were very low and consequently an outdated steam ship, the *Carl*, had been put on the passenger-route to Bornholm. The coal- or peat-driven *Carl* became the most important means of transportation of the illegal so-called *Lise-route*. At this time the USAAF were unaware that Bornholm was part of Denmark. According to the maps of their airmen the island belonged to Sweden. Consequently, the first crews of American aircraft emergency landing or crashing on Bornholm believed they had landed on neutral ground and that they were safe. When they realised they were on a quasi-hostile island they were facing uncertain

Roy's emergency-visa for Sweden. Source: private archive.

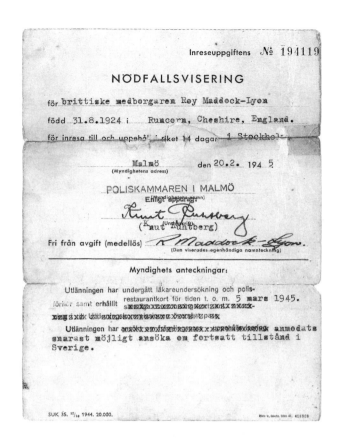

alternatives of arrest by Danish police or German forces or rescue by members of the Resistance movement. When, subsequently, assistance to allied crews forced to land on Bornholm was being better organised, the *Lise-route* carried quite a few allied airmen to Sweden. Roy, however, and other allied flyers (but not Jimmy and Jim) on their home-run were put onboard the *S/S Carl* from Copenhagen in order to jump off to the pilot boat escorting her through the Falsterbo Canal. The *Lise-route* owed its existence to a deal between the Swedish military authorities, the shipping line and its captain, and a Danish Resistance group.

The *Carl* departed from Havnegade on 19th February at nine p.m. More than three hours earlier – as soon as it was dark, but before German sentries controlled the embarkment of passengers – Roy was smuggled on board. He was instructed to hide behind a lifeboat on the top deck on the seaward side. At departure the *Carl* would turn 180° around and then Roy was to crawl to the opposite side of the lifeboat to avoid being exposed to the searchlight used by the watch ashore. It was freezing cold to lie there as a blind passenger for several hours without being allowed to move. Ordinary passengers embarked at eight p.m., being asked to show their identity cards. The number of German passengers, military or naval personnel, was usually high. All passengers, whether Danish or German, had to remain downstairs in the cabin and all windows and portholes had to be blacked out. Nobody whosoever was allowed on deck through the Falsterbo Canal. It was mandatory to take on board a Swedish pilot sailing in his own boat. This boat went alongside the *Carl*.

Furthermore, in February '45 the Swedish authorities had limited the number of German passengers in uniform to five. Virtually all doors were locked. Only the captain and two crewmembers were allowed to move freely. In other words no passenger could witness the coming and leaving of the pilot boat. The reason for this was that the Falsterbo Canal was Swedish military territory and defences were placed along the shores. When entering the canal a Swedish pilot boat came alongside the steamer and the pilot would be in charge during the passage. The pilot boat also brought Swedish military inspection on board the Danish ship. This was the moment when illegal passengers safeguarded by the Danish captain could swop boats.

Why wasn't Roy an ordinary, illegal passenger? Because the troubles for passengers to Bornholm in general and for refugees in particular had increased. The Gestapo got more and more suspicious that the *Carl* was smuggling illegal passengers, and they initiated a strict control by demanding lists of passengers and by checking names of passengers who had to present their cards of identity at embarkation. The number of passengers embarking must equal the number of passengers disembarking. But the names and addresses of identity cards of passengers coming and going must also be the same. On 5th February the Gestapo exercised a particularly tight control causing a delay for the fifty-six passengers for

S/S Carl of Neksø, Bornholm, originally 'Carl von Linné', built 1884 in Norrköping, Sweden, since '38 owned by A/S Det østbornholmske Damp-skibsselskab, at full steam, at the quay at Havnegade. Please note the life-boats on the top-deck.
Source: S.R. No. 93:93, Handels- og Søfartsmuseet på Kronborg, Elsinore.

more than four hours and the Germans removed nine passengers in Co-penhagen. It was revealed that six passengers jumped over board at Fal-sterbo and the crew tried to cover up its services by claiming that it had been threatened with revolvers. After their safe arrival at Rønne another nine or ten of the remaining passengers appeared to be illegal. They were still in need of an escort to Sweden and made contact with the Resistance on Bornholm. In other words: half the passengers were refugees or es-capees.

As a countermove against this fussy, yet futile control measure – which was also believed to comprise Danish informers – the organisers of the *Lise-route* launched a rather sophisticated scheme. This was made possible by the fact that the German sentries in the harbour of Copen-hagen were different from the ones at Rønne. Secondly, an escape in Falsterbo would result in a missing passenger when the ship arrived at Bornholm, so the pilot boat had to bring on board the *Carl* a substitute passenger in possession of an identity card with the same name (for the sake of the passenger list), but with the photograph of its bearer (for the sake of face control). Since the receiving controller had never set eyes on the passengers the swopping would remain undetectable.

In Roy's case these complicated measures were taken care of by Poul Prom, the translator and naval officer who was involved in *Elverhøj*. From his mobile office (at this time very close to Shellhuset) he would telegraph by means of a portable wireless – in code of course – all data from the identity papers of the escaper to Sweden. At that time the Germans had four stationary and seven mobile direction finders in Copenhagen alone, so communication with Sweden was risky, but mail by boat was often too slow, so urgent messages had to be radioed. However, no substitute passenger was available at that time for Roy. Consequently, he had to embark on the *Carl* not only as an illegal passenger, but as a blind one as well.

When the *Carl* had left the quay at Havnegade and all passengers had been locked up below deck the captain ventured to bring Roy into his cabin and offer him egg and bacon, tea and toast. Roy, however, crept straight into the captain's berth for want of warmth. When thawed out he fully appreciated the tea. At midnight he was called up on deck and shown on board the pilot boat taking him ashore where a British envoy, the Military Attaché, awaited him with legal Swedish papers. Poul Prom had advised the British Embassy in Stockholm of Roy's arrival. Roy did not know that then, but it was vital for him to have an emergency visa to enter Sweden, for, otherwise, the Swedish officials would have had to intern him. Roy Maddock-Lyon was no longer Mr. Peter Jensen, but had regained his own identity.

Roy shared the train compartment of the night sleeper to Stockholm with a courier from Berlin who brought messages to his embassy just as Roy was carrying letters to his. Roy in the top bunk, the German in the bottom. The train driving on neutral territory the German did not bother to know details about his travel companion. In Stockholm Roy was presented with a carton of Gold Leaf Virginia cigarettes by the Air

Attaché who interrogated him in great detail about his escape route and his helpers. The report, however, was tacit on names. It only mentioned that 'A' did so and so, 'B' lived at this and that address, etc. It was forwarded to MI-9 in London immediately. Routine procedures were strictly obeyed, even if the risk of the report to end up in enemy hands seemed minimal. But it did exist. For instance, the Germans might shoot down the aircraft carrying it. This would jeopardize several Danes. After a few days, Roy who had been chain-smoking asked for another carton of cigarettes to calm down his nerves. It was denied him.

✳ ✳ ✳ ✳ ✳

Jimmy, it will be remembered, was left safely with Professor Richard Ege in Copenhagen. Rev. Johannesen had already provided him with Danish identity papers, so he was ready to be smuggled into Sweden whenever an opportunity arose. Saturday 17th he left Richard's flat followed by a distant escort who guided him to the dock area. The escort was probably Jan Weber, a doctor working for *Speditøren* – another escape route. There was some delay, because the plan was to get Jimmy on board a ship together with two freedom fighters searched for by the Gestapo, and the escort were waiting for them. Eventually they boarded the *Clytia*, a small coaster. The refugees were directed into a small compartment in the bilges, so they clambered into this confined space. The door was now bolted and the outer compartment was filled with water. They waited a fairly long time in fish stench and complete darkness when they heard sets of footsteps on the deck. Some guard and his dog were inspecting the vessel. They did not stand a chance of detecting the three evaders below deck. The water and the stench of fish covered up their scent.

The *Clytia* left the harbour in the evening of 17th February, and when some hours later when the skipper found himself to be in safe water off the Swedish coast, the tank was pumped out and the three passengers crawled, out covered in fish oil and slime. Jimmy had landed at Varberg at midnight only three days after he had baled out. The Swedish police locked him up in the police station for the night, to interrogate him the next day.

He was then interned in a cluster of buildings outside Stockholm, which proved to be a quarantine camp. He was soon transferred to a refugee camp housing a large number of Danish refugees. They were all put to work. Every day they were sent outside the camp to chop wood for the boilers preparing their food and to cut ice for refrigeration. Jim spent about two weeks there and was then sent to the British Embassy to be fitted out with decent clothes. While waiting for a plane for England, he called Jim, who was reported to be at the airport, to learn that he had been on stand-by for a flight for five successive nights, only for the flights to be cancelled. He expected these delays would continue. Nonetheless, Jim got a flight home that evening, and Jimmy followed a few days later. After his safe landing in Sweden, Esther and Paul received a phone call informing them that 'the potatoes had arrived in good condition'. They did not recognize the voice.

M/S Clytia, a schooner built in 1896 at Thurø, owned by different people, in '45 by a Holbæk skipper. This photograph was taken in 1960 at Norrtälje, Sweden.
Source: S.R. No. 82:90, Handels- og Søfartsmuseet på Kronborg, Elsinore.

The Mills family and little Wanda, summer '45.
Source: private archive.

Jimmy arrived in England on 10th March – two months before the birth of his first child, a little girl, born on 10th May. She was baptized Wanda. Two of her father's helpers, Esther and Vera, had sewn a number of handkerchiefs for his first-born child. The material they used was the white silk from her father's parachute.

After his return Jimmy renewed his contract with RAF, but retired in 1951. Since then he has earned his living as a lorry driver in London.

✷✷✷✷✷

On the morning of 17th February Jim was met by Georg Suhr, the former policeman, and taken to the flat of Erik Poulsen and his wife, Edel, Under Elmene 12, Amager, directly opposite a police station occupied by the Germans. George and his wife Ruth also lived in that flat on the third floor. From the windows they watched the German sentries parading. Jim was furnished with an identity pass. Now he was John Hansen, a bookbinder by trade. He was also deaf and dumb, but, fortunately, nev-

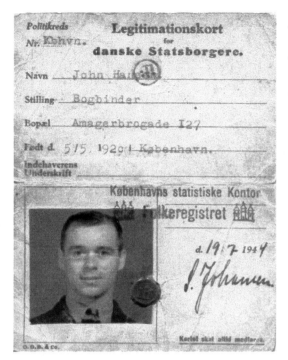

Jim's identity card: Book-binder John Hansen, false address, correct date of birth.
Source: private archive.

er put to the test. Instead followed nine quiet days of reading English books while waiting for a passage to Sweden. Sometimes Jim and George would go out to see people and sometimes they noticed RAF aircraft overhead as they were passing over to bomb the enemy in Germany.

Why did it take so long to obtain a shipping opportunity to Sweden? To give an idea of the difficulties involved in keeping this escape line going let me quote an extract from a contemporary letter of 3rd March '45 from *Speditøren*, the network in question, well-known for its high degree of security. One of its leading members stands out by name, i.e. Aage Skjoldby, who may be the person writing the following to Ejnar Andersen, a police constable, handling affairs on the Swedish side.

'Let me try to give you an impression of the circumstances behind a passage these days to enable you to appreciate how six adults can spend all their time sending a number of refugees to Sweden. *Pluto* departed a week ago, as you know, carrying ten persons. It sounds easy, but the intention was that she should have departed from the provincial harbour (Korsør) Monday noon. It was only to moor alongside the quay for two hours, so we had to be present.

So, we gathered the ten refugees Saturday afternoon. This lasted the whole afternoon since we could not make them stay at home all day. Monday morning we left at five o'clock a.m. Two escorts are necessary to manage them. As they arrive at the harbour the boat is not there. We wait for her the whole day. Accommodation in town is unprocurable, so, we have to send them back home again by the last train. The next morning at five a.m. the same people set out again. Yet, once again the boat has not come. They wait another full day. The weather forecast announces fog. Still the boat does not arrive. No accommodation. They must be sent back again. Two refugees have not arrived on time. One of our men must wait. The two refugees arrive just on time to watch the train leave. Still no accommodation to be found. They find an empty weekend cottage and break a window. Here three people are sitting the entire night without blankets and mattresses. No light can be switched on, no fire can be lit. It was bitterly cold. In the morning they take the first train to Copenhagen. Once again ten refugees depart from Copenhagen. They reach the harbour and this time find that the boat has arrived, too. Finally we can put on the list: Ten refugees shipped. *Pluto* was scheduled for departure from here the following Monday (26th), so we worked Monday, Tuesday, Wednesday and in the end had everything ready for Thursday. The boat had to be at quay on Wednesday in a harbour decided by us to enable us to bring on board the refugees during the evening and night. She only arrived on Thursday at three o'clock p.m. and had to depart immediately. Consequently, we had to put fifteen people on board in broad daylight. Three of these were disabled.

One man had to be transported by bike, which was done successfully apart from the arrival of a Gestapo patrol of sixteen men ready to fire their machine guns exactly at the time we came biking with the disabled man. He attracted their utmost interest, but as at the same time our man started screaming loudly and flinging his arms around we made it. What we could not make was averting the gale which had started in the meantime. Hence *Pluto* only departed today. This, in all modesty, is a slight lamentation.'

Source: Aage Skjoldby's archive, RA, Copenhagen.

Such were the circumstances at the time Jim was awaiting shipment. The sea of the Sound was too rough for smaller boats to meet from both sides. Besides German inspection had been intensified. Hence provincial harbours were occasionally preferred to Copenhagen and small harbours along the shore of the Sound. Jim's transport had been requested for the first time on 19th February, when *Speditøren* called the other side to ask them to notify Jim Petre's wife that her husband was safe and would join her shortly. She was worried, of course, having been informed by the RAF that her husband was missing. Something went wrong, however, and Mrs. Petre only received the happy message from Roy's parents during the first week of March.

During February '45, however, *Speditøren* was lucky to find a new skipper who was willing to and capable of carrying out illegal shipments to Sweden. This was the 'Dagmar', whose owner converted his fishing vessel to a boat for a very limited number of passengers completely undetectable, or so it seemed. The skipper emptied the fresh water tank of his boat, cut a whole in it big enough for an adult to crawl through and into a hollow space between the tank and the ship's side. This tiny room contained four people capable of closing the cutout hatch from their hiding place just outside. The tank was then refilled and the entire ship ready for German inspection including dogs, which stood a very poor chance of retrieving the secret load. Security was first class.

The last two nights before embarking the *Dagmar* Jim was taken care of by Aage Peterik, Næstvedgade 10, one of *Speditøren*'s helpers. Finally, on 28th February Jim together with three Danish refugees was escorted to Tuborg Harbour where the harbour master, Johannes Johansen, introduced him to his fellow passengers. They were Bodil Kjer, Ebbe Rode, and Mogens Wieth, three highly estimated actors of the Royal Theatre in Copenhagen. Bodil Kjer and Ebbe Rode were married to one another, and Mogens Wieth was their close, mutual friend. Their sympathy for the struggle for freedom was no secret; as a matter of fact, the Resistance were worried about their security, especially because the two men were fond of provoking the Germans in public, just as Mogens was renowned for his outspoken anglophile attitude and excellent command of the English language. In February '45 the Resistance found it was high time to remove the three actors to safety in Sweden. It was set about that the Gestapo on suspicion that they were funding the armed struggle for freedom wanted them. Hence they went underground, but none of them were initiated to the planning of the flight let alone who was going to carry it out.

The four passengers were placed on board the *Dagmar* in the narrow space across the width of the fishing boat between the water tank and the ship's side. Sitting four people together in this opening about 18" wide was most uncomfortable but none of them were expecting to travel first class. Before they cleared the docks Germans boarded the vessel on two occasions and flashed their torches. It was a dreadful sea crossing due to high winds and heavy seas. Bodil had put on as many clothes as she could possibly wear. Then the horrors of seasickness turned up, and confined as they were, vomiting over the rail was out of the question. Jim remembers Bodil as a very beautiful woman, but her mascara ran due to seasickness and tears, which she vividly remembers, too. Sikker-Hansen, the skipper, requested help from the Swedish coastguard but it was not forthcoming. Eventually they landed in Landskrona.

The three actors went quickly ashore and were welcomed, whilst Jim remained in the cabin. Mogens returned with a message from the Swedish police that Jim was to be interned for the duration of the war. Unwilling to put up with that, Jim demanded to speak to the nearest available British Consul. Fortunately he lived at Hälsingborg, only twenty

Telephone :

Gerrard 9234

Extn 3800

Any communications on the
subject of this letter should
be addressed to :—

THE
UNDER SECRETARY
OF STATE,

and the following number
quoted :— P.428627/6/B.3.B.

Your Ref.

AIR MINISTRY,

(Casualty Branch),

73-77, OXFORD STREET,

W.I.

23rd February, 1945.

CONFIDENTIAL

Sir,

I am directed to convey to you the good news that your
son, Sergeant Roy Maddock-Lyon previously reported missing, is
now safe.

A report has been received from a reliable source through
the Air Attache Stockholm which states that your son will be
arriving in Sweden shortly.

In the interests of your son you are asked to keep this
good news to yourself and not attempt to communicate with him
in any way.   This information should not be released to the
press.

I am to assure you that any further news received will be
passed to you immediately.

I am, Sir,
Your obedient Servant,

J. R. Drury

for Director of Personal Services.

S. Maddock-Lyon, Esq.,
18, Victoria Road,
Runcorn,
Cheshire.

*Letter from Casualty Branch, Air Ministry of 23.2.45 to Roy's parents.
Source: private archive.*

18. Victoria Road,
RUNCORN.

28th. February, 1945.

Dear *Mrs. Petre*,

As the Mother and Father of the
Flight Engineer (Sgt. Roy Maddock-Lyon) of the
aircraft in which your husband was operating,
may we extend to you our best wishes for the
safety of your husband.

At the same time we hope you will
have received the good news, (as we have that
Roy is safe) that your husband is safe, and to
you we extend our hopes that the time will
soon be here when all the boys are back at
home once more.

Our thoughts have been with you
since we received the news - 'Failed to return'
and the anxious intervening time, as Roy
often spoke of the happy time he spent with
the crew.

Yours sincerely,

S. Maddock Lyon

Letter from Roy's father of 28.2.45 to Jim's mother.
Source: private archive.

Bodil Kjer and Ebbe Rode from the back, and Mogens Wieth from the front.

miles away, and when he heard about the idea of interning Jim, he laughed and said, 'Stand by, I'll be back in a matter of minutes.' Meanwhile the three actors were given split peas. This dish, undoubtedly, was meant to be a hospitable gesture by the Swedes. Nevertheless, appetite was modest. Saying farewell to his newfound friends Jim marvelled at how quickly Bodil was restored to beauty.

The *Dagmar* brought back the mail and the good tidings from Ejnar Andersen that all four refugees had landed safely in Landskrona on 1st March. At Hälsingborg Jim stayed two nights at a hotel where the Consul had his suite of offices. He was still wearing his old clothes provided by Lars Peter, so he requested a change and was provided with a great coat and a trilby hat by the Consul who, with typical British generosity, found that his suit and boots were presentable enough. He was then put on a train for Stockholm and met Bodil, Ebbe, and Mogens on the same

Bodil Kjer and Ebbe Rode surrounded by freedomfighters, both pictures from the film 'Den usynlige Hær' ('The Invisible Army'), Palladium, 1945. Source: Archives of the Danish Film Institute, Copenhagen.

train. Bodil was accommodated at a boarding house in Stockholm where she was bored to death. Ebbe joined *Den danske Brigade* (Danish troops trained in Sweden to fight in Denmark in case of an Allied invasion or a German collapse). His soldierly courage and his skill in the use of arms, however, were scarcely comparable to his talent as an actor. This couple were among the first to leave Sweden after the liberation. Their presence at the Royal Theatre was badly needed, since Oscar Wilde's 'The Importance of Being Earnest' was about to be staged. Copenhageners were starving for comedy.

Mogens Wieth was flown to Britain where the Special Operations Executive recruited him for a Jedburgh-team. These Jedburghs were meant to be trained to become liaison officers between the Danish Resistance movement and allied officers during the final phase of the war, when it might be difficult to predict German reactions. For instance it was considered dubious whether German officers would surrender to Danish freedom fighters. A Jedburgh-team would consist of four members: a British, an American and a native officer as well as a wireless operator. However, the advances made by Field Marshall Montgomery during the final phase of the war happened so quickly that the plan of dropping Jedburgh-teams in Denmark never came to anything. Mogens Wieth, therefore, heard the declaration of capitulation at Hatherop Castle, where his training took place, and when he returned to the euphoria of liberation in Denmark, he joined a group of British officers to repatriate the German troops.

Jim arrived by Dakota at Leuchars, Scotland, on 7th March, leaving Jimmy behind for another three days. Having no passport Jim was given the luxury of V.I.P. treatment: passed through customs quickly, given a Spartan supper, and allocated a bunk bed. The next day he was accompanied to Edinburgh railway station by a Warrant Officer and handed over to two Army Sergeants carrying rifles. When he wanted to go to the toilet he was escorted by both men, one on each side. Jim began to wonder how they would find a seat for three, but was told, 'Don't worry. We have a private compartment, including everything.' During the journey to London, Jim dozed off to sleep once in a while, but every time he opened his eyes he found them watching him. And when at King's Cross Jim said he needed a wash and brush up his guards agreed they would do likewise. Jim gradually realised that they were heading for MI-9 in St. John's Wood which proved to be the case. Upon entering the MI-9-building a Corporal on desk duty exclaimed 'Welcome home, Sir!', which rather puzzled the army boys, and continued, 'You must be hungry, go and have breakfast, by which time the Adjutant will be in his office'. According to their papers, apparently, the two guards had escorted a deserter from the RAF, and when the Adjutant made them aware of Jim's recent fate, they both apologized but defended their attitude by the suspicious looks of Jim's old clothing. The main point of his escorts had been to prevent him from talking to anyone and not to divulge names of his underground helpers.

After debriefing in a very relaxed atmosphere Jim was returned to his airbase at Melbourne where he was warmly welcomed. His next duty was to visit the parachute packing division to find the person who had packed the chute that saved his life when he was forced to bale out near 'Hjortholmsgaarden'. A girl from Women's Army Auxiliary Corps then produced a book showing her signature on the line where the number of Jim's parachute was listed, and he offered his grateful thanks. After leave Jim was re-crewed to bomb Helgoland in daylight. As the airmen relaxed on the grass awaiting to be called forward a red light was sent up from the flying control tower and they were informed by the wireless-operator that the flight was cancelled. More than that, the war was over, and the Germans had surrendered. It was the 5th May. The bar was immediately thrown open in the afternoon and the good tidings were celebrated the whole evening and night.

ALLIED CASUALTIES IN DENMARK

During the German occupation of Denmark 1940-1945 nearly three hundred allied aircraft crashed or were shot down over Danish territory or waters. They were crewed by roughly two thousand allied airmen. The Resistance movement rescued almost one hundred of these men. Via Sweden, they made the home run and resumed the struggle against Nazi-

Memorial Service for Johnny Grayshan and 'Red' Berry, buried at Østre Kirkegård (as well as for J.G. Cox og R.H. Dawson, buried at Tveje Merløse Kirkegård) in the chapel of Skt. Nikolaj Kirke, Holbæk, 26.8.45. To the left in front of the altar Rev. Laurberg-Jensen and to the right Rev. Kenneth Morgan, RAF.
Source: The Resistance Museum, Copenhagen, photo by Christian Meld-gaard.

Germany. Another sixty-eight RAF-pilots were rescued at sea by Danish fishermen and repatriated. But out of a number of approximately three hundred airmen forced to leave their aircraft in parachutes and landing alive about two hundred were apprehended either by Germans or by Danish authorities, sometimes tipped off by law abiding citizens, only to be handed over to the German occupying forces and turned into POWs. About 1700 were killed in Danish airspace or waters. Of these roughly 500 were drowned, while 1160 flyers, i.e. 1026 British and Commonwealth, and 134 American, were found killed on Danish territory by Germans or Danes and buried in this country with or without ceremony.

This piece of micro-history serves to illustrate a couple of points of the macro-history of the German occupation of Denmark, points that tend to be overlooked. It shows that in spite of the intentions declared by the Danish Government, the nation was inevitably dragged into the Second World War in Europe. Denmark could not proceed as an insular or even neutral country because its airspace was an important part of the theatre of war. Danish territory was a necessary stepping-stone for the German occupation of Norway and to a certain extent a useful starting point for German air raids on northern Britain. Later on, when the fortunes of war had turned, allied raids on Germany often needed to cross Danish airspace. The population of Denmark was pushed into this air war by providing soil, resources, and labour for the construction of airbases for the Germans. The Danes were also involved in the air war when airmen landed alive, and all of a sudden, locals were facing the individual choice of handing them over to the enemy or assisting them on their home run.

Denmark was an important asset to Germany in its struggle against the Allies. The collaboration with Germany put the Danish authorities under the obligation to surrender Allied airmen for imprisonment. The fact that Governmental authorities surrendered approx. two hundred flyers, while the Resistance movement rescued approx. half that number, places Denmark in a state of vassalage under Nazi-Germany, although with scattered pockets of disobedient citizens. In this respect the micro-story is out of proportion, in so far as only two crewmembers (Stan and

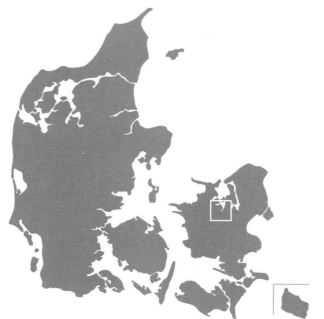

Map of the site of the crash:
  0. Hjortholmsgaarden, the site of the air duel.
  1. Old people's home 'Søgaard', the site of the crash.
  2. The blacksmithy belonging to Karl Petersen, Sønder Asmindrup.
  3. The vicarage of Rev. Paul With Johannesen, Sønder Asmindrup.
  4. Smallholder Ejner Næsholt Sørensen, Søby.
  5. Smallholder Johannes Helms, Havremarken.
  6. Doctor Vilhelm Schlippe, Sønder Jernløse.
  7. The grocer's shop, Vinstrup.
  8. German antenna mast, Mørkemosebjerg, and farm occupied by German air defence warning service, Græsmarken.
  9. The spot in Maglesø, where the female informer was dumped on 2nd Febr.' 45.
  10. Marup Enge, where Jim landed in his parachute.
  11. Smallholder Lars Peter Larsen, Skovager, Rye.
  12. Count F.C.R. Scheel's estate, Ryegaard.
Source: N.H.R. Scheel's archive.

111

Andy) were handed over to the Germans, while three of them (Roy, Jimmy and Jim) made the home run. According to average, many more than two of the Halifax-flyers would have been killed right away, and only one third of the airmen would have made an evasion, if we take the liberty to ignore the sixty-eight rescued by fishermen (since they were often picked up outside Danish waters).

Hopefully, this story demonstrates that the war split the nation. There was no longer a national community, if there ever were one; talking about 'we – the Danes' made no sense. When Allied airmen descended through Danish airspace they landed in hostile territory; nobody in the divided nation could escape an individual commitment to the war in Europe. This story of seven airmen as told by five of them has also substantiated how demanding and how perilous it was for the Resistance movement to show solidarity with Allied flyers. On the other hand it substantiates the double standards of the Government, since its politics were not only carried out as collaboration, but were virtually directed against the Allies. Yet, the political establishment joined in the euphoria as the Allies liberated the country.

SOURCES

A large part of the evidence has been provided by *interviews* I have taped and written *reports* by and *correspondence* with the five still surviving crewmembers. This evidence has been held up against contemporary *British archival material* whenever possible. Alan Thomas, Air Historical Branch, Ministry of Defence, has kindly sent photocopies of interrogation reports by the Air Ministry and MI-9. Tom Thackray, 10 Squadron Association, Guildford, and Duncan Stuart, CMG, SOE Adviser, Foreign & Commonwealth Office, London, have given valuable advice (thanks to K.J.V. Jespersen, Syddansk Universitet for establishing contact).

On the Danish side I have interviewed Johannes Helms, Havremarken, before he passed away, as well as his children Agnete, Niels Ebbe and Peter Andreas. All helpers were much older than the young airmen and are no longer alive. Hence I have been in contact with their children: Ingrid (the daughter of Ejner Næsholt Sørensen) N.H.R. Scheel, Ryegaard, (son of Count F.C.R. Scheel), Jørgen Hellemann, Borup (son of L.P. Larsen's daughter), Lise Lyngstrøm (daughter of Nina and Carl Syrach-Larsen), Brita Gottschalck (daughter of Minna og Christian Meldgaard), Karen With Kaas (daughter of Esther and Paul With Johannesen). I have also been lucky enough to find eyewitnesses: Helen Larsen, Vipperød, Esther, born Jeppesen, Holbæk, Margrethe Bahn Larsen, Holbæk, and Herlev Hjortholm Nielsen, 'Hjortholmsgaarden' near Nyrup. Rev. Paul With Johannesen wrote various contemporary reports (to which the writer Michael Clasen, Vipperød, drew my attention). So did Christian Meldgaard, and Brita Gottschalck, his daughter, kindly lent them to me. There are a number of newpaper articles on the event, but generally their reliability is poor. Rev. Carsten Barsløse, Holbæk, has kindly given me access to a number of obituaries kept by Skt. Nikolaj Church, Holbæk, and Jørgen Junker, Riisskov, has shared his impressive knowledge of the Luftwaffe with me. Thanks to E.H.V.Jensen, Flyvestation Karups Historiske Forening, for clarifying technical problems and for loan of photographs. I have had the opportunity to discuss details with a number of freedom fighters: Kurt Petersen, Midtsjællands Folkeblad, Poul Hyttel, a member of the former local committee of Danmarks Frihedsråd, Holbæk and DKP, Viggo Dreyer, Havnsø, H. Schmidt, Frøslevlejren, Gunnar Dyrberg, 'Holger Danske', Jørgen Jespersen, BOPA, Ole Lippmann, SOE. Bodil Kjer has kindly let me interview her on her escape by the 'Dagmar' to Sweden. Finally, I have profited from talking to a number of colleagues: Flemming Sylvest, Holbæk, Peter Øvig Knudsen, Weekendavisen, Nils Bredsdorff, Roskilde Universitetsbibliotek, Therkel Stræde, Syddansk Universitet, Carl Axel Gemzell and Hans Hertel, Københavns Universitet, as well as the architects Jens Johansen, Elith Juul Møller, Dea Trier Mørch, and Mogens Boertmann.

The following *Danish archives* have been used:
Allied airmen, F-10, Frihedsmuseets Arkiv, Civ. Ing. Tage Bertelsen's report on Luftwaffe's defence organisation in Denmark of 8.9.45 to the Intelligence Agency of the Military Command, Frihedsmuseets Arkiv, Aage Skjoldby's Archive, RA, 'The Sound Services" Archive, RA, Poul Prom's Archive, RA, Anders Bjørnvad's Archive, RA, Refugee Administration, Register of Englishmen buried in Denmark, and Church Services, Documents relating to English and American Soldiers buried in Denmark, RA, John Christmas-Møller's Archive, RA, Holbæk Politi, Political Charges 1945, LAS, F.O. Nielsen's Archive, Holbæk Lokalhistorisk Arkiv (Peter Blumensaadt), and for *photographs*: The Archive of The Danish Film Institute, Copenhagen, Holbæk Museum (Lene Floris) and Jernløse Lokalhistoriske Arkiv (Peter Korsgaard), Ebbe Falster, Copenhagen, and Jens Peter Petersen's photo album in private archive.

The following *literature* has been useful:

Gebhard Aders, *Geschichte der deutschen Nachtjagd 1917-1945*, Stuttgart, 1977.
Jørgen H. Barfod, *Et Centrum i Periferien. Modstandsbevægelsen på Bornholm*, Rønne, 1976.
Besættelsens Hvem-Hvad-Hvor, Politiken, 1966.
Victor Bingham, *Halifax – second to none*, Airlife, 1986.

Anders Bjørnvad, *Hjemmehæren. Det illegale arbejde på Sjælland og Lolland-Falster 1940-45*, Odense Universitetsforlag, 1988.

Anders Bjørnvad, *De fandt en vej*, Odense Universitetsforlag, 1970.

Claus Bundgård Christensen, Niels Bo Poulsen og Peter Scharff Smith, *Dansk arbejde – tyske befæstningsanlæg*, Blåvandshuk Egnsmuseum, 1997.

Alan W. Cooper, *Free to Fight Again. RAF Escapes and Evasions 1949-1945*, Airlife, 1988.

Henrik Dethlefsen, *De illegale Sverigesruter 1943-45. Studier i den maritime modstands historie*, Odense Universitetsforlag, 1993.

M.R.D. Foot and J.M Langley, *MI9. Escape and Evasion, 1939-1945*, London, 1979.

'Danske Arbejderes Skæbne i Tyskland', *Frit Danmark*, February, 1944.

Victor F. Gammon, *Not All Glory! True Accounts of RAF Airmen Taken Prisoner in Europe 1939-1945*, London, 1996.

William H. Garzke, Jr. and Robert O. Dulin, Jr., *Battleships. Axis and Neutral Battleships in World War II*, Naval Institute Press, Annapolis, Maryland, 1990.

Helge Gram, Et døgn i besættelsestiden, *Norsk Militært Tidsskrift*, 1984.

Helge Gram, Skudt ned over Danmark 1940-1945. Allierede flyvere satte livet på spil for vores frihed, *Frihedsmuseets Årbog*, 1999.

Birger Hansen og Ove Hermansen, Allierede Nedstyrtninger i Sjællandsområdet 1939-45, *Flyvehistorisk Tidsskrift* 2-88, 1988.

Jahrbuch der deutschen Luftwaffe, 6. Jahrgang, Leipzig, 1940.

Knud J.V. Jespersen, *Med Hjælp fra England*, bd. 1, Det lange Tilløb 1940-43, Odense Universitetsforlag 1998, bd. 2, Den væbnede kamp, 1943-45, Odense Universitetsforlag 2000.

Henrik Skov Kristensen, Claus Kofoed, Frank Weber, *Vestallierede luftangreb i Danmark under 2. Verdenskrig*, Aarhus Universitetsforlag, 1988.

K.A. Merrick, *The Handley Page Halifax*, Aston Publications, 1990.

Gordon Musgrove, *Operation Gomorrah. The Hamburg Firestorm Raids*, London, 1981.

Aage Nørfelt, *Usporlige veje*, Odense Universitetsforlag 1993.

Carsten Petersen, *Luftkrig over Danmark*, bd. iii, Jagerkontrol 1943-45. Karup 1940-1945, Ringkøbing, 1988.

Carsten Petersen, *Luftkrig over Danmark*, bd. iv, Jageroperationer, Ringkøbing, 1989.

Carsten Petersen, *Tyske Fly i Danmark 1940-45*, bd. ii, Natjagere, Ringkøbing, 1993.

Carsten Petersen, *Tyske Fly i Danmark 1940-45*, bd. iii, He 111 og Ju 88, Ringkøbing, 1996.

Alan Hjorth Rasmussen, *Det er nødvendigt at sejle... Nordsøfiskeriet under 2. Verdenskrig*, Fiskeri- og Søfartsmuseet, Esbjerg, 1980.

Michael Salewski, *Die deutsche Seekriegsleitung 1935-1945*, bd.iii: Denkschriften und Lagebetrachtungen 1938-1944, Frankfurt am Main, 1973.

P.Chr. v. Stemann, *En dansk Embedsmands Odyssé*, bd.i, København, 1961.

Therkel Stræde, 'Arbejderbevægelsen og Tysklandsarbejderne', in *Årbog for Arbejderbevægelsens Historie,* 1994, p.159-188.

Ditlev Tamm, *Retsopgøret efter besættelsen*, København, bd. 1-2, 1984.

Christian Zentner and Friedemann bedürftig, *Grosses Lexikon des Dritten Reiches,* München 1985 (articles: Junkers, Kriegsgefangene, Organisation Todt, Volkssturm).

Translation. Finally, I would like to thank Dorte Heurlin, Eric Routley, and Bill Buchman for their generous help in improving my English. For remaining flaws I alone am to blame.